THE BALTIMORE SUN
Where Maryland Comes Alive.™

www.sunspot.net

Terps: National Champions is a joint publication of
The Baltimore Sun Company and Sports Publishing, L.L.C.

TERPS: NATIONAL CHAMPIONS

SPORTS PUBLISHING, L.L.C.

Publisher: **Peter L. Bannon**
Senior Managing Editors: **Joseph J. Bannon, Jr. and Susan M. Moyer**
Art Director: **K. Jeffrey Higgerson**
Coordinating Editors: **Scott Rauguth and Erin Linden-Levy**
Graphic Designer: **Kenneth J. O'Brien**
Book Layout: **Jennifer L. Polson**
Imaging: **Joseph T. Brumleve**

THE BALTIMORE SUN

Publisher and CEO: **Michael E. Waller**
Editor: **William K. Marimow**
Managing Editor: **Anthony F. Barbieri**
Deputy Managing Editor/Sports: **Stephen R. Proctor**
Assistant Managing Editor/Sports: **Sam Davis**
Deputy Sports Editor: **Steve Marcus**
Product Manager: **Tony Burke**

Hardcover ISBN: 1-58261-570-5
Softcover ISBN: 1-58261-522-5

CONTENTS

THE BALTIMORE SUN
Where Maryland Comes Alive.™

www.sunspot.net

Dear Terps Fans,

The season got off to a shaky start last November 8. Maryland opened the year at Madison Square Garden with a 71-67 defeat at the hands of Arizona. But, boy, did it change quickly. The Terps reeled off eight straight wins before losing at Oklahoma and five more consecutive victories before falling to archrival Duke.

But Juan Dixon, Lonny Baxter and Byron Mouton and company would lose only one more time, against North Carolina State in the Atlantic Coast Conference Tournament, before winning Maryland's first national basketball championship and posting a 32-4 record.

As the NCAA tournament opened, coach Gary Williams' Terps had defeated Duke handily in the rematch, won the ACC title with a 15-1 record and gained a No. 1 seed in the East Regional. And the best was yet to come.

After defeating Sienna in the opening round, Maryland rolled past five former NCAA champions—Wisconsin, Kentucky, Connecticut, Kansas and Indiana—to become national champion in its own right.

Sun reporters and photographers were there from Day 1 to capture the excitement, drama and celebration of Maryland's greatest basketball team and the crowning achievement of coach Williams' distinguished career.

We are proud to present their work and Maryland's story in this book.

Michael E. Waller

Michael E. Waller
Sun Publisher

Terps Hope to Begin As Well As They Ended

by GARY LAMBRECHT

In the eyes of Maryland Terrapins senior center Lonny Baxter, the path promises to be challenging, yet the task is simple.

The time for feeling good about the men's basketball team's first Final Four trip in school history has passed. The time for putting every ounce of energy into winning Maryland's first national championship has begun. And there is no room for a bad stumble or a traumatic emotional swing. That bumpy path defined the Terps last season, beginning with a 1-3 start and continuing with a midseason 1-5 slide that threatened to knock Maryland out of the NCAA tournament for the first time in eight years.

"The biggest challenge is to win it all. The biggest challenge is ourselves, and how badly we want it," said Baxter, who will combine with senior shooting guard and fellow preseason All-American Juan Dixon to form Maryland's backbone.

"We know we have the potential. We know we have the right players. Basically, the same team is back. We have to start the season the way we ended it last year. If we start it like we finished it, we'll pretty much be unstoppable. I can't wait for the first day of practice."

Neither can coach Gary Williams, who officially gets his 13th year in College Park—and Maryland's last season at Cole Field House—rolling with the annual Midnight Madness event at 12:01 a.m. on Saturday.

There is no time to waste. Four weeks from Thursday, the Terps open on the earliest date in school history by facing Arizona in the Coaches vs. Cancer Classic at Madison Square Garden in New York. The winner plays the Florida-Temple winner on Nov. 9, with the losers playing in the consolation round the same night.

Williams loves the sense of urgency that the schedule forces as much as he likes this team's chances to win an Atlantic Coast Conference title and advance beyond the national semifinals, where Maryland lost to Duke in Minneapolis on March 31.

ANDRE F. CHUNG, THE BALTIMORE SUN

Ten players, including four starters, return from the 25-11 squad that regained its footing with a flourish, winning 10 of its final 12 games. Both losses came against Duke, the popular preseason pick to win another title.

The Terps have been tabbed by several publications as a top three team. As for another fall marked by high expectations, Williams seems bored by the question. After all, Maryland has won 120 games since 1997, the most prolific five-year stretch in the program's history. The Terps have been to five Sweet 16 rounds in the past eight years.

"I think it's a natural progression for our program to be picked high in the preseason," Williams said. "All Maryland people should stop asking that question [about dealing with high expectations]. That question has to stop, if we want to be a consistent program."

What remains to be seen is whether the Terps can add firepower after subtracting it, and whether they can wear down opponents with tremendous depth again.

Gone are key components from the frontcourt, which was the deepest in the nation last year. Power forward Terence Morris now plays for the Houston Rockets. Small forward Danny Miller, unhappy with his playing time, transferred to Notre Dame, leaving the starting job to senior Byron Mouton, who replaced Miller last December. Backups Mike Mardesich and LaRon Cephas have left.

"With Terence, we lost a very good rebounder who gave us 25 minutes a game. Danny was an exceptional defender who gave us 19 minutes. Mike was a physical presence who gave us 10," Williams said. "We've got some things to work on."

The offense, one of the game's most explosive a year ago, will flow through Baxter in the low post and Dixon up high again, with point guard Steve Blake back as a third-year starter and looking to improve on his 6.9-point scoring average.

Baxter erased some regular-season problems with a furious finish. He won the MVP of the West Regional by dominating the big men from Georgetown and Stanford. Dixon (team-high 18.2 points) was one of the toughest defenders in the ACC who kept finding ways to score, be it off turnovers, by getting to the foul line or burning teams with medium- and long-range jumpers.

"Great players know they can't stay the same. They have to get better. I think Juan is a better ball handler now," Williams said. "And he really wants to prove that he's still a winner."

Backup Drew Nicholas returns with experience at both guard positions, and freshman point guard Andre Collins should add to the depth with his quickness.

The biggest question marks loom among the bigger guys. With Miller gone, will Mouton avoid foul trouble and be more consistent with more minutes coming his way? And at power forward, will Tahj Holden and Chris Wilcox create a powerhouse position? Holden is a physical presence with a deft shooting touch. Wilcox, maybe the best pure athlete on the team, who has bulked up to 230 pounds, could be the breakout player in the ACC.

Newcomer Ryan Randle could push his way into the rotation. With Miller gone, freshman Mike Grinnon figures to see notable playing time behind Mouton.

Williams will never forget the Terps hitting rock bottom last February by losing at home to last-place Florida State. That dropped Maryland to 15-9. The Terps then rebounded all the way to Minneapolis.

"We want to remember the feeling of going to the Final Four. We want to remember the feeling of losing five out of six, that sinking feeling that our season was sliding away," Williams said. "Both of those things should be motivators."

ELIZABETH MALBY, THE BALTIMORE SUN

Win Over Temple Restores Terps' Confidence

Williams Glad to See UM Bounce Back After Opening Loss to Arizona

by GARY LAMBRECHT

They are a veteran group that already has proved itself in the postseason heat of March, yet the team's 82-74 victory over Temple did wonders for a Maryland Terrapins squad that needed to believe in itself once again.

The signs of Maryland's maturity stuck out in many ways. One night after losing in lackadaisical fashion against Arizona, which followed up by beating Florida to win the Coaches vs. Cancer Classic as the tournament's only unranked squad, the Terps rediscovered a sense of urgency their fiery coach wore on both nights, as he stalked the sideline in Madison Square Garden. After Arizona frustrated them with a matchup zone and seemingly beat the Terps to every key rebound and every loose ball, Maryland refused to stand still against No. 16 Temple.

The Terps forced the issue, countering Temple's famed matchup zone by forcing an up-tempo pace and hitting the outside shots they missed so frequently 24 hours earlier. Their frontcourt hit the boards vigorously, even though its stalwart, senior center Lonny

Baxter, watched much of the proceedings while sitting with foul trouble. They overcame a horrendous early showing at the foul line, making their final 12 free throws after missing 10 of their first 16 attempts. They took charges, dug deep into their bench to wear down the Owls, and never lost their composure.

And on a night when Temple point guard Lynn Greer was a scoring machine—his 27-point effort, which included a 30-footer among his three late three-point baskets that kept the Owls within striking distance—the Terps answered again. And again. To the tune of 59.1 percent shooting, including 63.2 percent from three-point range.

Senior guard Juan Dixon led the way with 25 points. Just as notable was junior point guard Steve Blake, who erased a bad night against Arizona point guard Jason Gardner by drilling the Owls for a career-high 20 points on near-perfect shooting. Blake missed only once while sinking four threes, four foul shots, seven attempts overall and burning Temple for 15 points in the second half.

NATIONAL CHAMPIONS

All of which was enough to bring the first regular-season smile to coach Gary Williams' face.

"Every year, I don't care where you're ranked or who you have back [from the previous year], you've got to win against a good team. Then, you have confidence," said Williams, who should pass his former coach, Bud Millikan, to take over second place in school history with his 244th victory against American on Saturday.

"There are a lot of teams out there who are good and well-coached, but they're just not good enough to beat Temple. Shooting 59 percent against that defense is pretty good. It was intense out there. If you don't play that way against a John Chaney team, you don't win. We know we can win now."

The Terps avoided the school's first 0-2 start in 39 years, and are a virtual lock not to repeat last year's season-opening, 1-3 start. After playing the Nike Elite team in an exhibition at Cole Field House on Tuesday, Maryland will play host to American and Delaware State on back-to-back Saturdays, before facing visiting Illinois in an ACC/Big Ten Challenge showdown on Nov. 27.

"We want to go on a straight road this year," said Dixon, who played through a sprained left ankle against Temple and finished the tournament with 46 points and nine assists and made 10 of 20 three-point shots. "We have a heck of a team, and we want to show it each and every night."

Said Blake: "We were all pretty down after the Arizona game. We knew we needed a victory to get excited about our season. That's what we did. Everyone's confidence is up right now."

The Terps were equally tough and resourceful on their second try. Instead of going with a seven-man rotation as he did against Arizona, Williams expanded the roster by introducing reserves Calvin McCall and Ryan Randle to the action.

McCall, who helped to form a three-guard alignment, hit a three-pointer that gave the Terps an early 13-12 lead against the Owls. Randle helped Maryland maintain a three-man rotation down low that included Tahj Holden and Chris Wilcox. With Baxter out of the game so much, the Terps needed that trio to perform. Randle contributed two points and three rebounds in his Division I debut.

"At first, I was shocked. That's my first time playing in Madison Square Garden. I've seen it on TV, and I thought one day I'm going to make it there," Randle said. "As soon as coach said get in there, all of my butterflies went away. I feel wonderful."

So did Holden and Wilcox, especially after coming up empty on the defensive boards in the opener. Friday night was a different story. They combined for 13 rebounds, including nine on the defensive end.

Holden, who made his first collegiate start, had five points, two assists, two blocked shots, took two charges and forced a tie-up that allowed Maryland to maintain an important, late possession. Wilcox had seven points, a career-high nine rebounds and two assists. As a team, they stayed aggressive and eventually forced Ron Rollerson, Temple's nimble, rotund, 6-foot-10 center, to foul out with 9:12 left.

"We didn't play as well as we could or as hard as we could [against Arizona]," Holden said. "That was our focus against Temple."

JEFF ZELEVANSKY, AP/WIDE WORLD PHOTOS

JEFF ZELEVANSKY, AP/WIDE WORLD PHOTOS

"We knew we needed a victory to get excited about our season. That's what we did. Everyone's confidence is up right now."

Terp Junior Point Guard
Steve Blake

UM Too Good for No. 2

Dixon, Blake Guard Home Streak, Lead Terps by Illini, 76-63

by GARY LAMBRECHT

They were quicker, more aggressive, more inspired, and the Maryland Terrapins were not about to let their precious home-court advantage go to waste.

No. 5 Maryland made a memorable, early-season statement at sold-out Cole Field House by taking control of No. 2 Illinois in the first half, leading for the final 30 minutes, and wearing down the Fighting Illini, 76-63, in the opening game of the third ACC/Big Ten Challenge. In what was their most impressive effort of a young season, Maryland (4-1) won its fourth straight game by handing the Fighting Illini (5-1) their first loss, and the Terps did it the way they love to do it best—with a grinding, attacking, half-court defense setting the tone.

Maryland looked like a team that had thought long and hard about the way it lost to Illinois a year ago in the Maui Invitational. This time, while beating the Fighting Illini for the third time in four games over four years, the Terps were not about to be pushed around on the boards, and their guards refused to allow a fine Illinois backcourt to dictate the action.

The surprisingly easy victory—over an Illinois squad that was three nights removed from three games in three days in the Las Vegas Invitational—started with Terps guards Juan Dixon and Steve Blake, who thoroughly outplayed the Fighting Illini duo of Frank Williams and Corey Bradford.

Dixon scored a game-high 25 points, adding five rebounds and two steals. He also put the clamps on Bradford, who shot 4-for-14 and finished with eight points. Blake scored 10 points and added nine assists and a career-high four blocked shots, while harassing Williams to the tune of 3-for-16 shooting and 10 points. That had much to do with the Terps leading by as many as 20 points early in the second half.

"Teams are coming after us this year, and we have to go out there and give a great effort each and every night," Dixon said. "We showed people tonight that we want to win big games. It sends a message to everybody to watch out for Maryland. And me and Blake want to be considered one of the best backcourts in the country."

NATIONAL CHAMPIONS

How impressive were the Terps? They got a combined seven points out of their starting frontcourt of Lonny Baxter and Tahj Holden, both of whom fouled out. And it didn't matter, since 6-foot-10 sophomore forward Chris Wilcox came off the bench and was far too much for Illinois to handle. Mixing in an assortment of slams, baby hook shots and short jumpers, Wilcox burned Illinois with a career-high 19 points and added six rebounds and two blocked shots.

"I love being the spark off the bench," Wilcox said. "I can see a lot of things out there on the court, and when I get out there, I know what to do."

Maryland coach Gary Williams, who countered Illinois' three-guard alignment effectively and won that battle because reserve guard Drew Nicholas (season-high 12 points) played his best game of the season, said it all started with defense. And the clinic started after Illinois had taken a 17-10 lead. When the night was done, the Fighting Illini had shot just 36.7 percent from the field.

"Defensively, when we look at a team as good as Illinois, we look for a way to shut them down," said Williams, whose Terps maintained the nation's longest nonconference home-court winning streak at 80.

"When you look at their scoring and what they did last year in terms of balance, you can't just take away Bradford or Williams and say we have them stopped. Team defense starts with each player stopping their man, like on the playground. We depended on our ability to play head-up, man-to-man defense. We really worked hard tonight."

Although they got out-rebounded, 42-38, the Terps—who were beaten by 18 rebounds a year ago by Illinois—dominated the boards while they were taking control in the middle of the game. They tossed people to the floor, ran through people to get to loose balls, and made the Fighting Illini look slow for much of the evening.

And only some glaring free-throw shooting problems in the second half kept this from being a runaway Maryland victory. After falling behind early, 17-10, Maryland outscored Illinois 31-12 over the final 13 minutes of the half to take a 41-29 lead at halftime.

Wilcox and Nicholas combined for 17 points in the first half and fueled the turnaround. Dixon then made a three-pointer, a short jumper and a layup after his own steal, as the Terps opened the second half with a 10-2 run to take a 51-31 lead.

During a stretch in the middle of the second half, Maryland missed six of nine foul shots, while the Fighting Illini, behind Bradford and Damir Krupalija (10 points), crept to within eight points twice. But after Maryland's lead slipped to 66-58 with 2:56 left, the Terps regrouped. Wilcox started a clinching run with five consecutive points to make it 71-58, and Maryland was never threatened.

"Wilcox just owned us inside. I think he's great," Illinois coach Bill Self said. "They've got a really good team."

"**Teams are coming after us this year, and we have to go out there and give a great effort each and every night.**"
TERPS GUARD JUAN DIXON

ELIZABETH MALBY, THE BALTIMORE SUN

November 27. 2001: Illlinois vs. MARYLAND

	1st	2nd	Total
Illinois	29	34	63
MARYLAND	41	35	76

Illinois

Player	FG-FGA	3-PT FG-FGA	FT-FTA	O-D REB	A	BLK	S	TP
34 Cook	3-5	1-1	1-2	1-6	0	1	0	8
21 Archibald	3-6	0-0	2-4	4-6	3	2	0	8
13 Bradford	4-14	0-5	0-0	2-1	2	0	2	8
24 Harrington	2-3	2-3	0-0	0-0	1	0	0	6
30 Williams	3-16	1-5	3-4	0-4	1	0	1	10
00 Melton	0-0	0-0	0-0	0-0	1	0	0	0
04 Head	1-2	0-1	0-0	0-1	0	0	0	2
23 Ferguson	2-6	0-1	7-8	1-2	1	0	2	11
25 Howard	0-0	0-0	0-0	0-0	0	0	0	0
33 Krupalija	4-7	1-2	1-2	4-4	2	0	0	10
43 Powell	0-0	0-0	0-0	0-0	0	0	0	0
45 Smith	0-1	0-0	0-0	0-0	0	0	0	0

MARYLAND

Player	FG-FGA	3-PT FG-FGA	FT-FTA	O-D REB	A	BLK	S	TP
01 Mouton	1-3	1-1	0-0	1-2	2	0	1	3
45 Holden	1-4	0-2	0-0	2-4	3	1	2	2
35 Baxter	2-7	0-0	1-4	1-4	1	1	0	5
03 Dixon	9-19	2-8	5-6	2-3	1	1	2	25
25 Blake	3-7	2-3	2-4	0-4	9	4	1	10
12 Nicholas	5-8	1-2	1-2	0-4	1	1	0	12
33 Randle	0-2	0-0	0-0	1-1	0	0	0	0
54 Wilcox	8-13	0-0	3-8	2-4	1	2	0	19

NATIONAL CHAMPIONS

LONNY BAXTER/ JUAN DIXON

Inside Out, a Tough Shell

by GARY LAMBRECHT

Juan Dixon smiled as he heard himself describing his role on the last basketball team he will play for at the University of Maryland. Dixon, a slender, 6-foot-3 shooting guard from East Baltimore, who could become the first Terrapin since John Lucas to earn first-team all-Atlantic Coast Conference honors three times, was relishing his senior status and the authority it brings. When asked by a reporter about the locker-room hierarchy in the final year at Cole Field House, Dixon said the Terps belong to him this year.

Then, as he spotted 6-8 senior center Lonny Baxter sitting across the room talking with more media members, Dixon corrected himself.

"I would say this is mine and Lonny's team. He's my big fella. He might grab me and throw me in a hamper in the locker room if he reads that I said it's my team," Dixon said.

"I worked hard to get where I'm at, along with Lonny. This is the first time me and Lonny have a chance to be leaders. We can show the young guys what it takes, because we know what it takes."

The little man and the big man bring an intriguing set of differences and similarities to the court, starting with the way each player began at Maryland as a lightly regarded local prospect and has long since silenced the skeptics.

Dixon, a Calvert Hall alumnus who overcame the AIDS-related deaths of both of his parents, was said to be too small and weak to mix it up effectively in the ACC. He needed to sit out as a redshirt in 1997-98 just to get stronger. But don't mistake the 164-pound Dixon's skinny legs and bony shoulders as signs of weakness. He has the lowest percentage of body fat on the team, and pound for pound, Terps strength coach Kurtis Shultz said, he is the strongest player in the weight room.

Baxter, who is from Silver Springs, had problems with weight and discipline as he played at several Washington-area high schools before spending a year at Hargrave Military Academy. Look at him now and you see a chiseled, 260-pound, all-ACC force who sets the tone for a physical front line that should be a prominent part of Maryland's identity this year.

"It's really been amazing to watch Juan and Lonny develop as players and as people," Williams said. "People thought Juan was too skinny, and it was hard to tell the athletic ability Lonny had before he developed his body. He was a little heavy, but he made up his mind to be good. If Lonny and Juan didn't have that work ethic, they wouldn't be this good."

"In their sophomore years, they weren't focal points of the offense. They just played hard and played well," ssaid Tahj Holden, the Terps' 6-10 junior power forward. "Now things go through them. You've got to get the ball to

Lonny first to open up the outside. Then get it to Juan outside and everything starts clicking.

"Lonny is really confident right now. He knows nobody can stop him in practice. Juan is probably one of the most confident people I know. He's never satisfied."

The big man and the little man complement each other well. Baxter controls the low post with brawn and quickness and some of the best power moves in the land. He showed the nation what a beast he can be on the blocks during Maryland's memorable run through the NCAA tournament last spring, as Baxter destroyed the front lines from Georgetown and Stanford to earn the West Regional's Most Valuable Player award.

"Three seasons under my belly has really helped me a lot. I used to be overweight, not in shape, just learning the game," Baxter said. "Juan and I used to hear people say, 'Why did Maryland recruit them?' We used that as motivation. Determination is what got us here."

"I worked hard to get where I'm at, along with Lonny. ... We can show the young guys what it takes, because we know what it takes."

TERPS GUARD JUAN DIXON

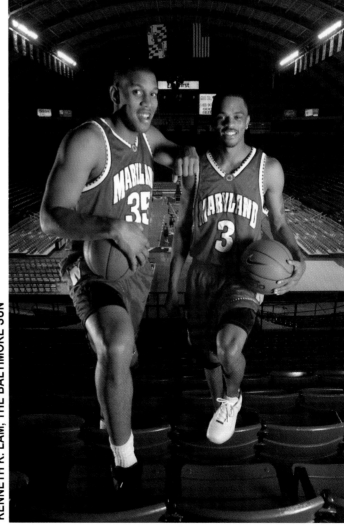

KENNETH K. LAM, THE BALTIMORE SUN

25

Princeton Tests Terps' Patience

No. 5 Prevails, 61-53, but Needs to Rally

by GARY LAMBRECHT

They started the day by playing their worst half of the season, and their incompetence drew a chorus of boos as they left the MCI Center court at halftime.

But the Maryland Terrapins, so ineffective early against a disciplined, deliberate Princeton team that worked the shot clock artfully and ran its offense flawlessly, showed the mettle of a No. 5 team by turning a 13-point halftime deficit into a 61-53 victory in the opening round of the seventh BB&T Classic. Maryland (5-1), which won its fifth straight and advanced to the tournament title game against Connecticut, suspected it would be in for a testy day against the unranked Tigers. And the Terps were right.

They were a mess in the opening 20 minutes, making only seven baskets, missing nearly half of their free throws and committing 12 turnovers. They were determined to stop Princeton from getting open for three-point shots and backdoor layups —Princeton trademarks. Maryland could stop neither, as it fell behind at intermission 36-23, marking the lowest scoring in an opening half since the

Terps managed 19 points in their NCAA tournament loss to St. John's in 1999.

"I think we kind of fell into their trap in the first half," said Maryland senior center Lonny Baxter, who led all players with 19 points and 12 rebounds, marking the 25th double-double of his career.

Yet Princeton (1-4) could not prevent Maryland's size and talent from asserting itself in the second half, as the Terps stuffed the Tigers by allowing just 17 points.

Maryland gave up two points off only four second-half turnovers, worked the ball relentlessly inside, crushed Princeton on the offensive boards and finally was calm at the foul line. The Terps ended a glaring slump by making 14 of their last 17 free throws, as five different players contributed down the stretch. They made 22 of 33 overall, for a season-high of 66.7 percent.

Led by Baxter, who exploited Princeton center Konrad Wysocki's foul trouble, and senior guard Juan Dixon, who tied a tournament

---

NATIONAL CHAMPIONS

NATIONAL CHAMPIONS

record with six steals and scored nine of his 14 points with perfect shooting at the foul line, the Terps outscored Princeton 33-11 over the game's final 14:18. Maryland finished the Tigers off with a 10-2 run, after working for nearly 35 minutes to take the lead it relinquished after scoring the game's opening basket.

"The key is to get more patient, even though you're trailing. That's a hard thing to get across when players are nervous," said Maryland coach Gary Williams, whose team trailed at the break for the first time this season. "By halftime, the thought of losing was there. I wasn't sure we'd have enough time to come back. We're down by 13, and I know [Princeton] is going to take 25 seconds off the clock [with each possession].

"Princeton is no secret anymore. It's been a long time since they've been playing like that. To their credit, they were able to play the way they wanted to play in the first half. We were the best team in the second half, and we won the second half by more."

Maryland endured plenty of roadblocks. The Terps, who managed only three Baxter layups from the field in the game's first 11 minutes— Baxter also picked up three first-half fouls— came unglued by allowing a 19-9 Princeton run with a slew of turnovers over the final nine minutes of the first half.

Reserve forward Chris Wilcox, who scored six points and grabbed 11 rebounds, had some words with Williams on the bench after a sloppy stretch of play. And the Tigers punctuated their big opening when guard Ahmed El-Nokali hit a three-pointer as the shot clock expired to give Princeton a 36-23 lead with 30 seconds left in the half.

Princeton reached its high-water mark with a 42-28 lead with 14:18 left. Then, after Baxter scored on back-to-back layups and Dixon hit two free throws to make it 44-34, the 6-foot-8 Wysocki drew his fourth foul with 12:42 left. That left Baxter and Wilcox to roam more freely on the blocks, and it sparked Maryland for good at both ends of the floor.

After a tip-in by Wilcox, Drew Nicholas converted two free throws to pull Maryland to 44-38, and suddenly a new trend was born. Forward Tahj Holden followed another tip-in by Wilcox by making two free throws. Byron Mouton turned a midcourt steal into a layup, then made two foul shots to tie the game at 46 with 6:22 left. Nicholas gave Maryland its first lead since the opening seconds by hitting a three-pointer from the top of the key to make it 51-49 with 4:42 left.

Wysocki's slam briefly tied the score at 51, but a short jumper by Wilcox gave the Terps the lead for good. Over the final three minutes, Dixon, Mouton and point guard Steve Blake made all six free throws to put Princeton away.

"The key is to get more patient, even though you're trailing. That's a hard thing to get across when players are nervous."

MARYLAND HEAD COACH GARY WILLIAMS

December 2, 2001: Princeton vs. MARYLAND

	1st	2nd	Total
Princeton	36	17	53
MARYLAND	23	38	61

Princeton

Player	FG-FGA	3-PT FG-FGA	FT-FTA	O-D REB	A	BLK	S	TP
23 Bechtold	2-8	0-3	0-0	1-5	2	1	1	4
25 Logan	5-14	0-2	5-6	2-6	4	3	0	15
34 Wysocki	6-9	1-2	0-0	1-3	2	0	1	13
03 Wente	3-5	1-2	0-0	0-2	2	1	2	7
15 El-Nokali	2-4	2-3	0-0	0-1	2	0	0	6
10 Persia	0-0	0-0	0-0	0-0	2	0	0	0
22 Venable	0-0	0-0	0-0	0-1	0	0	0	0
30 Wallace	1-3	0-0	2-2	1-0	0	0	0	4
31 Robins	0-0	0-0	0-0	0-0	0	0	0	0
35 Martin	0-3	0-0	4-4	1-4	1	1	1	4

MARYLAND

Player	FG-FGA	3-PT FG-FGA	FT-FTA	O-D REB	A	BLK	S	TP
01 Mouton	1-4	0-1	4-5	1-4	0	0	1	6
45 Holden	1-4	1-2	2-2	0-1	1	0	0	5
35 Baxter	8-15	0-0	3-10	5-7	0	2	0	19
03 Dixon	2-9	1-4	9-9	3-0	2	0	6	14
25 Blake	1-6	0-1	2-2	0-1	8	1	2	4
12 Nicholas	2-4	1-3	2-2	0-2	0	1	0	7
33 Randle	0-0	0-0	0-0	0-0	0	0	0	0
54 Wilcox	3-8	0-0	0-3	6-5	1	2	0	6

Terps reach BB&T heights
Baxter, Holden Are Too Big for UConn in 77-65 Tourney Win

by GARY LAMBRECHT

The Maryland Terrapins had trouble shooting and handling the ball for glaring stretches of the game, but still had too many weapons for the Connecticut Huskies to handle.

Sparked by its frontcourt of senior center Lonny Baxter and junior forward Tahj Holden, No. 3 Maryland overcame the less experienced and unranked Huskies with an impressive second half and won its second straight BB&T Classic, 77-65, before 14,813 at the MCI Center. The victory, Maryland's sixth straight, gave the Terps (6-1) their fourth BB&T crown in the tournament's seven-year history and their third championship in the past four seasons. Maryland also became the first back-to-back winner of the BB&T in its history.

And the Terps needed their big men to put down Connecticut, which gamely battled its own ball-handling and shooting misery. The Huskies fell behind early by a 21-7 count, used their defense and transition game to cut that margin to 36-34 at halftime, then hit the wall—in the form of Baxter and Holden.

Baxter scored 14 of his game-high 24 points in the second half on perfect 4-for-4 shooting, and added 10 rebounds to record his second straight double-double and earn tournament MVP honors.

Holden, who played for much of the game in foul trouble on a night when reserve forward Chris Wilcox had the same problem, awakened from a season-long scoring slump to score a season-high 15 points, all in the second half. Holden recovered from an ineffective, 0-for-2 showing in the first half by making all four of his shots from the field after halftime. Terps guard Juan Dixon added 16 points, six steals and five rebounds, but was plagued by six turnovers.

Baxter and Holden, who also combined to make 12 of 14 free throws, were in the thick of Maryland's 18-6 run at the start of the second half. They scored 14 of the Terrapins' points during that stretch, as Maryland took a 54-40 lead with 12:44 left and never led by fewer than seven points after that.

NATIONAL CHAMPIONS

NATIONAL CHAMPIONS

"It feels a lot better. It feels like I helped out," said Holden, who entered the game averaging just 4.7 points. "I just found myself open a lot in the second half. Coach tells us to shoot the ball with confidence. [The Huskies] were doubling down on Lonny big-time, and I let the game come to me."

"Tahj hasn't been shooting the ball well, and I noticed on tape he's been taking shots when he's covered and not shooting when he's open," said Williams, who loved the way the Terps responded at halftime in each of their tournament victories.

The Terps trailed Princeton by 13 points at the break in Sunday's victory.

"We're not going to quit, I know that," Williams said. "It was a little shaky at halftime. We just sucked it up at halftime on both nights. That's good to see."

The Terps overcame a 20-point night by Connecticut forward Caron Butler, were beaten by 10 on the boards and committed 15 turnovers. But Maryland also threw down the hammer on the younger Huskies by forcing 20 turnovers and stifling an offense that was averaging 92.7 points in its first three games.

Maryland owned the game's first eight minutes, which featured a slew of Connecticut turnovers, a technical foul on coach Jim Calhoun, and the Huskies' inability to make a basket.

Sparked by Baxter, Maryland bolted to an 11-2 lead. Baxter began his night by converting a three-point play, two free throws, and a layup after grabbing an offensive rebound. When Dixon completed the game-opening run with two free throws at the 15:35 mark, Connecticut had missed its first five shots, committed five turnovers and Calhoun had been whistled for coming onto the floor to argue a no-call.

It got worse for the Huskies, as the Terps extended their lead to 21-7 with 12:10 left. Maryland scored eight unanswered points, with four different players scoring, during that spurt.

But after Calhoun had burned his second timeout, Connecticut rebounded by forcing some Maryland turnovers and beating the Terps down the floor in transition. Butler awakened the Huskies with a steal and a three-point play. Taliek Brown then added a fast-break layup, and suddenly the Huskies were off on a 13-0 run. Brown finished it by stripping Dixon and making a transition layup to cut Maryland's lead to 21-20 with 7:48 left.

The Huskies missed two chances to take the lead. The Terps never lost the lead, but they did cooperate by missing shot after shot and turning the ball over repeatedly. By the time the half mercifully had ended, the teams had combined for 24 turnovers and only 10 assists.

> "I just found myself open a lot in the second half. Coach tells us to shoot the ball with confidence."
> TERPS JUNIOR FORWARD TAHJ HOLDEN

December 3, 2001: Connecticut vs. MARYLAND

	1st	2nd	Total
Connecticut	34	31	65
MARYLAND	36	41	77

Connecticut

Player	FG-FGA	3-PT FG-FGA	FT-FTA	O-D REB	A	BLK	S	TP
03 Butler	7-19	0-1	6-6	5-1	2	0	2	20
44 Selvie	4-10	0-0	3-5	3-5	0	0	0	11
50 Okafor	3-6	0-0	2-2	4-8	1	2	2	8
12 Brown, T	2-8	0-0	0-0	1-2	2	0	2	4
32 Robertson	3-8	0-1	0-0	1-2	3	0	1	6
04 Gordon	3-10	3-6	1-2	1-0	2	0	2	10
20 Brown, J	1-3	0-0	0-0	1-1	0	0	0	2
21 Hazelton	1-5	0-1	2-2	1-3	0	0	0	4
25 Hayes	0-0	0-0	0-0	0-0	0	0	0	0

MARYLAND

Player	FG-FGA	3-PT FG-FGA	FT-FTA	O-D REB	A	BLK	S	TP
01 Mouton	1-7	0-2	0-1	3-2	1	0	0	2
45 Holden	5-7	1-1	4-4	1-1	0	1	1	15
35 Baxter	8-10	0-0	8-10	2-8	0	1	1	24
03 Dixon	5-18	2-7	4-4	1-4	3	2	6	16
25 Blake	3-8	0-3	2-3	1-0	9	1	1	8
12 Nicholas	3-6	0-3	1-3	0-1	2	1	1	7
33 Randle	0-0	0-0	0-0	0-1	0	0	0	0
54 Wilcox	2-6	0-0	1-2	4-5	0	3	0	5

NATIONAL CHAMPIONS

KARL MERTON FERRON, THE BALTIMORE SUN

CHRIS WILCOX

Terps' Wilcox on Rise; Look Out Below

by GARY LAMBRECHT

If Chris Wilcox is scary now, wait until he learns the game. In the meantime, as the student continues to study and digest the finer points of basketball, opponents might consider themselves lucky to contend with a force as unrefined as it is overwhelming. For now, Wilcox is a raw, muscular, 6-foot-10 sophomore power forward who comes off the bench with the ability to take over a game for the University of Maryland. He is a crowd-pleaser of the highest-flying order—a dramatic dunk, block or rebound waiting to happen.

When Wilcox leaves the bench at Cole Field House, he creates a buzz in the stands, as the home crowd anticipates the next Wilcox moment that could be destined for a television highlights package. But his biggest fans are his fellow Terrapins, who often during practice get to suffer the abuse of this 19-year-old with a potentially huge NBA future.

"The guy has crazy talent," senior guard Juan Dixon said.

"He can dominate whenever he wants," senior center Lonny Baxter added. "When you see some of the things he can do, you say, 'Oh my God, he's a couple feet over the rim.' It's amazing. When he really uses his talent, he's the best guy out there."

"When he gets the ball five feet from the basket, you just better hope the ball doesn't go in. When he's going to the rim with it, I'm getting out of the way," said junior guard Drew Nicholas. "I'm sure the guys guarding him in practice want to get mad sometimes, but then you have to say there's not much I could have done."

"Everybody wishes they could jump like him," said junior forward Tahj Holden, who starts and shares his position with Wilcox, while trying to contain him in practice. "Even Michael [Jordan] wishes he could jump like him now."

There might not be another sixth man like him in the league.

Look at the mark he made in his most telling performance. It happened Nov. 27 against visiting Illinois, then ranked No. 2.

With the Terps trailing 17-10, Wilcox entered the contest and took over with a spectacular assortment of rebounds, put-backs, hook shots and slams. He made the Fighting Illini look slow and flat-footed. His career-high 19 points propelled the Terps to a rousing 76-63 victory.

"Wilcox owned us inside," Illinois coach Bill Self said. "I thought he was great."

"Sometimes I surprise myself a little bit, but I know what's there," said Wilcox, his eyes dancing with a look of mischief. "I look forward to picking up my teammates. They like the intensity level I bring when I get in there.

"I didn't have a real big role on the team last year. I'm more confident in my game this year. I guess I just had to get on the coach's good side. The best way to get playing time is to get in good with the man."

That would be Terps coach Gary Williams, who is watching Wilcox—the only Maryland player from hoops-rich North Carolina on the Terps' roster—grow on a day-by-day, practice-by-practice basis.

Wiser Terps Reload After Shooting Blanks in Loss to Oklahoma

by GARY LAMBRECHT

Even a good team that considers itself a potential national champion has to recognize its limitations.

In the eyes of Maryland basketball coach Gary Williams, the No. 2 Terrapins were reminded of some painful and useful truths in their 72-56 whipping by No. 22 Oklahoma. While staggering to the finish line with their lowest offensive output since scoring 54 points in a victory over Wake Forest nearly five years ago, Maryland did just about everything wrong when it had the ball in its hands.

From layups to wide-open three-point attempts, the Terps missed too many shots, particularly in the second half, when they shot 32.1 percent and produced only 22 points in their weakest 20-minute display of the season. Maryland added to that misery by committing a season-high 21 turnovers.

What really galled Williams is how the Terps (8-2), facing a two-headed monster by playing their first true road game while also dealing with a 10-day layoff, lost their identity on a night when the shots weren't falling. As Oklahoma, mindful of Maryland's poor shooting outside, began to collapse a zone defense around senior center Lonny Baxter, the Terps stepped out of character and tried too often to beat defenders one-on-one.

Not a good move for a team that lives by the extra pass. Not a good move against an Oklahoma squad loaded with athletes who made the Terps look slow for much of the evening. Maryland recorded only four assists during an 11-turnover debacle in the second half, when the Terps panicked during the Sooners' game-closing, 20-7 run.

Baxter, the anchor of the offense, was no factor while taking a season-low five shots, and he did not help his cause by turning the ball over six times. The Sooners also took senior guard Juan Dixon out of the action. Dixon took only three shots in the second half and went scoreless over the game's final 19:20. It was an unusual breakdown by an

NATIONAL CHAMPIONS

offense that prides itself on creating good shots.

"We have to be a passing team. We went into the NCAA tournament last year with more assists than any other team. We have to get back to that," said Williams, whose team had its eight-game winning streak broken and came up 21 points short of its 77-point scoring average.

"We took too many quick shots and didn't stay within the offense long enough. [Oklahoma] was more athletic at every position except at [power forward] when Chris Wilcox was in the game. We have to rely on each other more, instead of going one-on-one. Oklahoma can do that. I'm not sure we can. We have to figure out a way to get the ball inside. You have to stay with what you do best."

While beating their first top-five team since taking down No. 3 Kansas nearly six years ago, the Sooners (9-1) took the swagger out of Maryland in other ways.

Sparked by 6-10 sophomore center Jabahri Brown—a transfer from Florida International who was playing only his fourth game in an Oklahoma uniform—the Sooners controlled the boards in the second half, grabbing 26 rebounds to Maryland's 14.

Brown had eight of his game-high 14 rebounds in the second half, helping the Sooners overcome their own shooting problems. Forward Aaron McGhee had 11 rebounds, eight after halftime, as Oklahoma killed the Terps with second and third shots.

Oklahoma did not need the brawling style that was its trademark a year ago. The Sooners used their quickness to take Maryland defenders off the dribble and beat the Terps to loose balls. It was an impressive show by a team that could be a major threat in March.

"There are some things we can work on," said Williams, who expects the Terps to learn from their mistakes and move on accordingly. "We're 8-2, and we've lost to two pretty good teams [Arizona and Oklahoma], one on a neutral court and one on their home court. You don't get carried away with one game."

> ❝ **We have to be a passing team. We went into the NCAA tournament last year with more assists than any other team. We have to get back to that.** ❞
>
> MARYLAND HEAD COACH GARY WILLIAMS

December 22, 2001: MARYLAND vs. Oklahoma

	1st	2nd	Total
MARYLAND	34	22	56
Oklahoma	36	36	72

MARYLAND

Player	FG-FGA	3-PT FG-FGA	FT-FTA	O-D REB	A	BLK	S	TP
01 Mouton	4-11	0-2	0-0	1-3	0	1	4	8
35 Baxter	3-5	0-0	3-5	1-9	2	2	0	9
03 Dixon	5-12	0-4	1-1	1-2	1	0	1	11
25 Blake	2-11	2-8	0-0	1-3	6	0	1	6
45 Holden	1-4	0-1	0-0	0-1	1	0	0	2
12 Nicholas	1-6	1-4	2-2	0-1	3	0	1	5
54 Wilcox	6-8	0-0	3-4	2-7	1	1	0	15

Oklahoma

Player	FG-FGA	3-PT FG-FGA	FT-FTA	O-D REB	A	BLK	S	TP
13 McGhee	5-15	0-1	6-9	6-5	2	0	1	16
21 Brown	4-5	0-0	0-0	3-11	2	0	2	8
02 Ere	6-16	3-7	4-4	0-7	2	1	1	19
04 White	2-4	0-1	3-7	0-0	6	0	1	7
10 Price	3-10	0-6	0-0	0-2	2	0	4	6
05 Detrick	3-10	0-3	0-0	1-4	0	0	1	6
24 Selvy	4-6	1-1	1-2	3-0	1	0	3	10
42 Szendrei	0-1	0-0	0-0	0-0	0	0	0	0

NATIONAL CHAMPIONS

It's Dixon to Rescue for Terps
Guard's Key Steal, Clutch Free Throws Finish Ga. Tech, 92-87

by GARY LAMBRECHT

For more than 39 minutes against Georgia Tech at Alexander Memorial Coliseum, Maryland shooting guard Juan Dixon was one of the main attractions.

But Dixon, one of the nation's premier players and the heart of the No. 4 Terrapins men's basketball team, was merely warming up for an amazing display over the final 31 seconds of a gutty, foul-laden 92-87 victory over the unranked Yellow Jackets. Without Dixon, the Terps might have fallen for the third straight year at Georgia Tech, which erased much of a 16-point Maryland lead in the first half, then cut a 12-point deficit to one in the second half and made the home crowd believe an upset was possible.

Maryland (13-2, 3-0 Atlantic Coast Conference), however, kept pace with Wake Forest atop the conference standings, won its fifth straight game overall, and set up Thursday's much-anticipated showdown at Duke on a positive note because the kid from Calvert Hall refused to let it happen any other way.

Dixon began his theatrical finish with 31 seconds left, as the Terps clung to an 85-83 lead and were in danger of losing it after center Lonny Baxter had committed a turnover by throwing an interior pass into the hands of Georgia Tech forward Robert Brooks.

After Brooks threw an outlet pass to Yellow Jackets point guard Tony Akins, Dixon swooped in behind Akins and stole the ball out of his left hand near midcourt. Dixon dribbled across the line, then lobbed a 40-foot alley-oop pass to forward Chris Wilcox, who beat Brooks to the ball before jamming it home for an 87-83 lead.

Dixon then finished the Yellow Jackets with another facet of his game by making four straight free throws in the final 10 seconds. It was quite an exclamation point to another superb effort.

Dixon, the second-leading free-throw shooter in the league (90.4 percent), finished with 26 points and 10 rebounds, both game highs. He also led Maryland with three steals and added four assists in 38 minutes.

NATIONAL CHAMPIONS

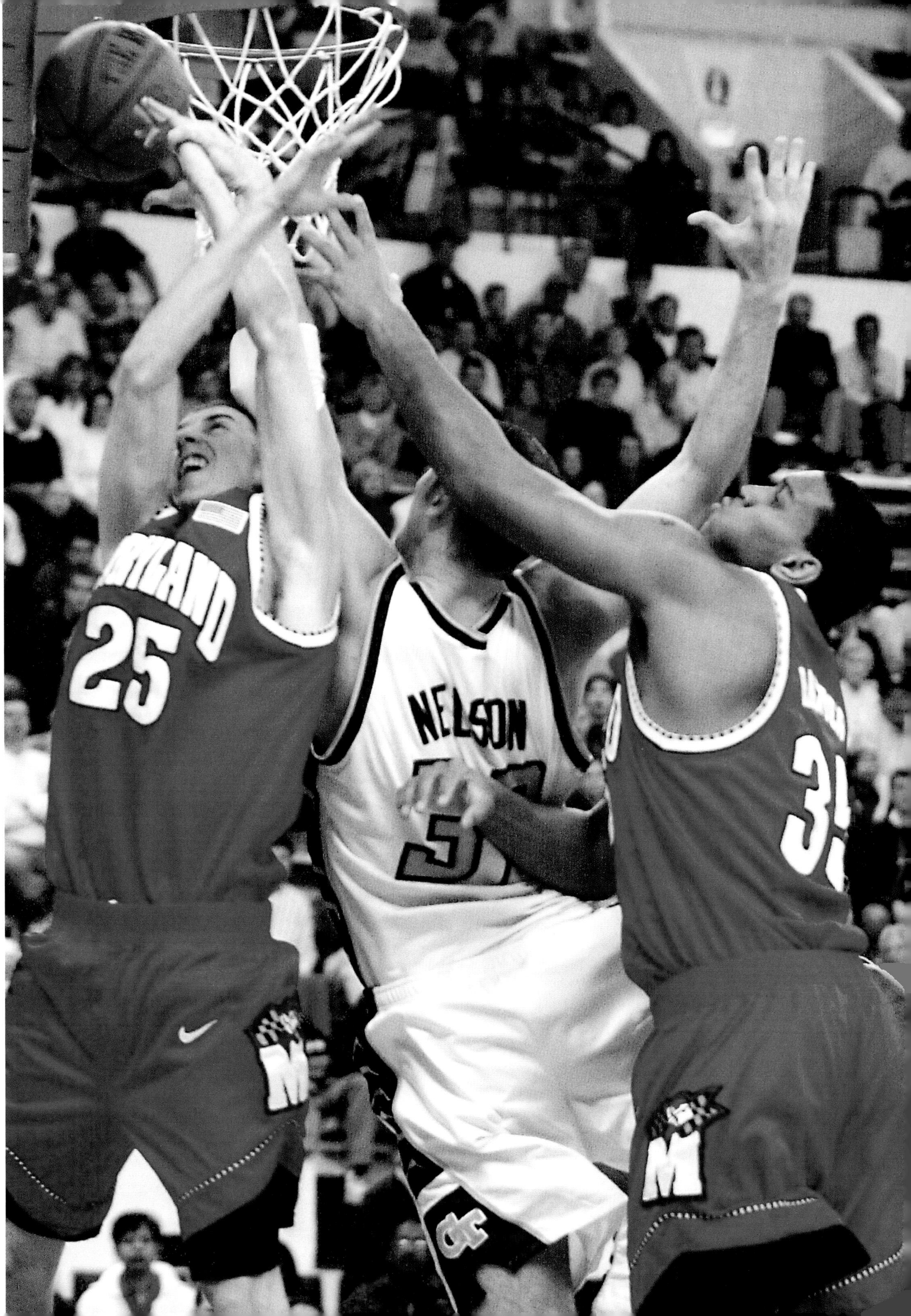

RIC FELD, AP/WIDE WORLD PHOTOS

Let the accolades begin, starting with Georgia Tech coach Paul Hewitt.

"Our effort was certainly worthy of winning, but we got beat by a great player who makes great plays in a lot of different ways," said Hewitt, who watched Dixon grab eight rebounds in the second half, make seven of eight free throws overall, and burn the Yellow Jackets with five three-pointers, including a couple from beyond 25 feet.

"If Juan Dixon is not making a three, he's making a great pass, or at the end there, it was him that made that steal," Hewitt said. "At the end of the shot clock he would knock down a shot or he'd make a play to get them an easy basket. He's a great, great player."

Said Maryland coach Gary Williams: "He's as tough as any kid I've ever had. He refuses to lose. That steal he made was an incredible play. He gets on the foul line and you just think he's going to make them. I don't say a lot of pretty things about my players or blow smoke about them. For what [Dixon] has done for Maryland, I don't think any player [in the nation] has had greater impact over the last four years on any team."

On a day when Maryland ran into foul problems that limited players like point guard Steve Blake (four points, five assists, seven turnovers in 25 minutes) and reserve forward Tahj Holden (three points in 21 minutes), and the Yellow Jackets (7-10, 0-4) belied their youth by effectively attacking the more seasoned Terps inside and got Akins loose outside in the second half for 16 of his team-high 24 points, Dixon closed the deal.

The Terps, who got 23 points from Baxter and 19 from forward Byron Mouton—each of

whom finished with four fouls while Blake fouled out with 20 seconds left—thought they would walk away with an easy victory after shooting 68 percent in the first half and taking a 48-35 halftime lead.

To its credit, Georgia Tech, which plays only one senior and no juniors, countered a 41-30 rebounding disadvantage and a 20-for-22 foul-shooting display by the Terps in the second half by playing a sharp transition game and by playing Maryland's game—pounding the ball inside to freshman forwards Ed Nelson and Isma'il Muhammad and sophomore forward Clarence Moore. They combined for 39 points and 20 rebounds.

Maryland answered a 6-0 Georgia Tech run to start the second half by pulling away to a 63-51 lead with 12:33 remaining, then got five straight points from Mouton after the Yellow Jackets had closed to 63-59 with 9:56 to go. Georgia Tech then forced two Maryland turnovers during an 8-0 spurt that featured back-to-back threes by Akins, cutting Maryland's lead to 68-67 with eight minutes left.

The game turned into a foul-shooting contest after that, and the Yellow Jackets showed their inexperience by missing five of eight attempts during a five-minute stretch, while the Terps protected their slim lead.

Then came Dixon's time to calculate and shine again.

"I don't think [Akins] saw me. I was creeping in behind him, baiting him," said Dixon, who moved into fifth place on the school's career-scoring list with 1,823 points. "I waited until he put the ball in his left hand, got that steal, and Chris [Wilcox] put the finger up [signaling for the lob pass]. That was a risky play. I saw him pointing and said, 'Should I throw it?' I prayed he would catch it."

Said Williams, with a grin: "[Dixon] knew he'd be dead if we didn't win. But that's what makes Juan what he is. He's got a lot of guts."

Added Baxter: "We knew this wasn't going to be a cakewalk. We got outworked in some rebounding and some loose-ball situations. But we got the win and Juan was huge. That steal, that's one of the things we had to have to win this game. It's one of those things that the great players do."

RIC FELD, AP/WIDE WORLD PHOTOS

January 13, 2002: MARYLAND vs. Georgia Tech

	1st	2nd	Total
MARYLAND	48	44	92
Georgia Tech	35	52	87

MARYLAND

Player	FG-FGA	3-PT FG-FGA	FT-FTA	O-D REB	A	BLK	S	TP
01 Mouton	7-10	0-1	5-6	0-3	4	0	0	19
35 Baxter	6-10	0-0	11-14	2-7	2	1	1	23
54 Wilcox	5-8	0-0	2-3	0-4	1	0	0	12
03 Dixon	7-16	5-10	7-8	3-7	4	0	3	26
25 Blake	0-2	0-2	4-4	0-1	5	0	0	4
10 Collins	0-0	0-0	0-0	0-0	0	0	0	0
12 Nicholas	1-4	1-3	0-0	0-0	4	0	1	3
33 Randle	1-2	0-0	0-0	0-5	0	1	0	2
45 Holden	1-2	1-1	0-2	0-4	1	0	0	3

Georgia Tech

Player	FG-FGA	3-PT FG-FGA	FT-FTA	O-D REB	A	BLK	S	TP
05 Moore	2-7	0-1	7-13	3-5	1	1	1	11
32 Nelson	6-9	0-0	6-10	1-7	1	1	1	18
34 Brooks	1-2	0-0	2-2	1-4	1	0	2	4
03 Akins	7-14	5-9	5-6	0-1	8	0	1	24
24 Lewis	4-10	3-6	1-2	1-0	3	0	4	12
01 Elder	1-1	0-0	0-0	0-0	0	0	0	2
02 Muhammad	4-6	0-0	2-5	1-3	2	0	0	10
33 Lane	1-7	0-3	2-2	0-1	1	0	0	4
55 McHenry	1-2	0-1	0-0	0-0	0	0	0	2

RIC FELD, AP/WIDE WORLD PHOTOS

STEVE BLAKE

Blake Keeps Terps On Point

BY GARY LAMBRECHT

Steve Blake remains hidden among the stars, and that's fine with him. Think of second-ranked Maryland, and the scoring and defensive gems of guard Juan Dixon spring to mind. So does the thought of center Lonny Baxter pounding away on the blocks, or forward Chris Wilcox soaring over everyone to grab one of those majestic rebounds or slam home a dunk. Blake? He is merely the junior point guard who delivers the spark that makes so much of it happen. He is merely the guy with the buzz cut, the game-face scowl and the nasty competitive streak who has kept the offense humming and kept the bigger names happy throughout this magical season in College Park.

For the second straight year, Blake has led the ACC in assists. This year, his 8.1 assist average overall ranks second in the nation. In league play, he is the leader with 8.8 assists a game, and his 2.9-1 assist-to-turnover ratio (2.5-1 in all games) also is tops in the ACC.

"Where would this team be without that guy?" Baxter said when asked about Blake's steadying hand in the offense. "An unselfish point guard is the best type of point guard, and he's always looking to get somebody else a better shot."

"He hates to lose at HORSE. He goes out and competes like that all of the time," said junior forward Tahj Holden. "You don't always need a scoring point guard, but you need guys like him to run your team. I can't say enough good things about him."

Blake chose diplomacy when asked about the number of people who have downplayed his contribution during his finest season at Maryland. Blake was named to the All-ACC third team, and you can hear a hint of resentment in his careful words.

"I really don't know how to look at it. I'm kind of disappointed," Blake said. "A lot of point guards you see today are scorers. I have a lot of scorers around me. As long as my team keeps winning, I'm happy."

Said North Carolina coach Matt Doherty: "There is probably not a coach in the country that wouldn't like to have him. Steve Blake deserves more respect than he got. The point guard to me is the most important position on the floor, and he is the point guard on the No. 1 team in our league. He makes that offense go. Such a great passer. Tough kid."

From the time he first saw him play, Maryland coach Gary Williams liked that tough kid, too. The way he dug in to play defense. The way he commanded his teammates while directing traffic. The way he exploited openings by taking only the right shot. The way he loved having the ball in his hands with the game on the line.

Blake had the right disposition for a baptism by fire, and that's what he got when Williams handed him the ball as a freshman out of Oak Hill (Va.) Academy. He took some early hits for the team. In his first BB&T Classic, Blake was handled by George Washington's Sir Valiant Brown. He battled early season injuries, and Maryland lost its first three ACC games.

By the end of the year, the Terps were a second-place, 11-5 team, and outside of Dixon, Blake was Maryland's most improved player.

"Every game was new, every building was new, every matchup was new and often was against a really good point guard. There's no way we win 20 games that year, let alone 25, without him," Williams said. "Steve looks like a veteran player now. He's stronger, and he's playing like an older player."

ELIZABETH MALBY, THE BALTIMORE SUN

Duke Runs Past UM

by **GARY LAMBRECHT**

Duke threw its trademark defense and the superb tandem of guard Jason Williams and forward Mike Dunleavy at Maryland, and the Terps were unable to answer after battling the Blue Devils basket for basket for much of the contest.

Top-ranked Duke turned a tense, much-anticipated Atlantic Coast Conference contest into a 99-78 rout over No. 3 Maryland before a sellout crowd at Cameron Indoor Stadium. The Terps, who were too sloppy with the ball down the stretch and suffered with an off night from star senior guard Juan Dixon, were unable to stay with the Blue Devils in the final 20 minutes after taking a 49-48 lead into halftime.

Williams had a game-high 34 points, while Dunleavy scored 19 of his 21 points in the second half, as the Blue Devils put together a game-ending 26-8 run after Maryland pulled within 73-70 with 10:28 to go. The Terps went without a field goal for nearly the final eight minutes.

Maryland (13-3, 3-1), which ended a five-game winning streak and was denied a chance to win its third straight game at Cameron, fell

apart in crunch time by committing a slew of its 21 turnovers. Dixon, guarded mostly by Duke forward Dahntay Jones, scored a season-low 10 points on 2-for-9 shooting. Dunleavy led all players with seven steals.

It was a deceptive finish to a game that featured 30 lead changes. Lonny Baxter led the Terps with 24 points and eight rebounds. Chris Wilcox had 14 points and seven rebounds. Duke center Carlos Boozer finished with 20 points.

Behind Williams, the Blue Devils (15-1, 4-1) used a 17-6 run over a five-minute stretch to take a 73-63 lead with 12:33 left in the contest. Williams scored nine points during that run. His three-point play made it 71-63, and a tip-in by Matt Christensen gave Duke a 73-63 advantage, which accounted for the biggest lead of the game at the 12:33 mark.

Maryland closed the gap to 73-70 with a 7-0 run, finished by a 12-footer by Drew Nicholas (12 points). But the Terps were unable to generate much offense after that.

After the Blue Devils opened by scoring the game's first five points, the first half turned

---

NATIONAL CHAMPIONS

BOB JORDAN, AP/WIDE WORLD PHOTOS

into a terrific shooting contest marked by constant lead changes.

Over the game's first four minutes, five Maryland players scored, as the Terps hit five of their first six shots. Duke, meanwhile, made seven of its first 10 attempts while taking a 16-15 lead with 15:45 left in the half.

Williams scored nine of the Blue Devils' first 16 points, most of them on drives through the lane. Maryland answered Duke's opening run with six unanswered points, capped by Dixon's three-pointer from the left corner to give Maryland a 6-5 lead.

From there, the lead would change hands 24 more times in the half, and the Terps would match the Blue Devils despite a quiet start by Dixon, who managed only six points by the break.

Williams' third driving layup of the game gave the Blue Devils a 13-12 lead with 16:40 left. Blake then answered with an off-balance three-pointer to give Maryland a 15-13 lead, but Williams came right back with a fast-break drive and layup, then converted a three-point play to put Duke on top once again.

Maryland, which worked the ball inside efficiently for much of the half to Baxter, Wilcox and backup center Ryan Randle, also got a lift from Byron Mouton. His pull-up, 15-footer in the lane put the Terps on top 21-20. After Daniel Ewing put Duke back on top with a 15-foot baseline jumper, Baxter—who led the team with 11 first-half points—hit a free throw to forge a 22-22 tie with 12:28 to go.

The Blue Devils, behind Williams and Boozer, then put together the best run of the half, a 13-5 spurt, to open up some breathing room. Once again, Williams was at the heart of the surge. His driving layup started the run. His put-back off of his own missed shot made it 31-24 with 10:18 to go. And after Baxter made a free throw and the Terps' Steve Blake banked in a 12-foot runner to cut the margin to 33-27, Williams made a 12-foot jumper to give the Blue Devils their largest lead at 35-27 with just under nine minutes left in the first half.

But Maryland, getting big contributions from Randle and Nicholas down the stretch, refused to go away. Wilcox and Dixon started the Maryland rally by combining on a 7-0 run to give the Terps a 36-35 lead with 6:20 left. Wilcox threw down a 12-footer to complete the run.

Nicholas then made his presence felt by scoring six Maryland points in a row. He grabbed an offensive rebound and converted a difficult six-footer, made a pair of free throws, then drove through the Duke zone defense for a layup to give Maryland a 42-41 lead with 3:22 to go.

At that point, there had been two ties and 20 lead changes, and still it went on. Boozer hit two free throws to put Duke back in front. Then Randle made a short jumper and converted a three-point play, giving Maryland a 45-43 lead. No matter. Jones made a three-pointer to put Duke back on top 46-45 with 1:05 to go.

Randle, who scored the last seven points of the half for Maryland, turned an offensive rebound into a layup to make it 47-46 in Maryland's favor. Randle then turned a perfect feed from Dixon into a layup and a 49-46 lead. But Jones sent the home crowd into delirium by banking in a 10-footer at the buzzer to trim Maryland's halftime lead to 49-48.

January 17, 2002: MARYLAND vs. Duke

	1st	2nd	Total
MARYLAND	49	29	78
Duke	48	51	99

MARYLAND

Player	FG-FGA	3-PT FG-FGA	FT-FTA	O-D REB	A	BLK	S	TP
01 Mouton	3-8	0-1	0-0	2-1	1	0	0	6
54 Wilcox	6-9	0-0	2-5	2-5	4	2	1	14
35 Baxter	8-14	0-0	8-15	4-4	1	3	1	24
03 Dixon	2-9	1-4	5-6	1-4	2	0	1	10
25 Blake	2-5	1-4	0-0	0-3	8	0	1	5
04 Badu	0-0	0-0	0-0	0-0	0	0	0	0
10 Collins	0-0	0-0	0-0	0-0	0	0	0	0
12 Nicholas	5-6	0-0	2-2	2-3	2	0	1	12
21 Grinnon	0-0	0-0	0-0	0-0	0	0	0	0
33 Randle	3-9	0-0	1-1	3-3	0	0	0	7
45 Holden	0-3	0-1	0-0	1-1	0	0	0	0

Duke

Player	FG-FGA	3-PT FG-FGA	FT-FTA	O-D REB	A	BLK	S	TP
30 Jones	4-11	1-4	0-0	1-0	0	2	0	9
34 Dunleavy	7-15	2-5	5-6	2-7	4	0	7	21
04 Boozer	6-10	0-0	8-8	1-4	0	1	0	20
21 Duhon	2-5	0-1	2-3	0-0	4	0	3	6
22 Williams	13-23	1-4	7-10	2-5	8	1	3	34
05 Ewing	2-3	1-1	0-0	0-3	0	0	0	5
15 Buckner	0-0	0-0	0-0	0-0	0	0	0	0
20 Sanders	1-2	0-0	0-0	1-0	0	0	0	2
41 Christensen	1-1	0-0	0-0	1-0	0	0	1	2
42 Love	0-0	0-0	0-0	0-0	0	0	0	0

BOB JORDAN, AP/WIDE WORLD PHOTOS

Maryland Gets Drop on Clemson

No. 3 Terps Overcome Tigers' 15 Threes, jump to 2nd in ACC, 99-90

by GARY LAMBRECHT

For a while, it seemed as if the shots would never stop falling for the Clemson Tigers. For a while, it seemed as if the Maryland Terrapins would miss too many free throws and lose too many rebounds to avoid losing their first home game of the season.

But the No. 3 Maryland men's basketball team, perhaps overcoming a hangover effect from a loss at top-ranked Duke, awakened in time to assert itself over the final five minutes and put away upset-minded Clemson, 99-90, before a sold-out Cole Field House. The crowd got quite an entertaining two hours for its money.

It witnessed Clemson's incredible shooting display in the first half, when the Tigers traded leads with the Terps by converting 11 three-point baskets to set a school record for most threes made in a half. It saw 10 different players score in double figures, including five from each team. It saw Maryland protect the ball as well as it has all season, while making the game's biggest shots.

And after Maryland had pulled away from the Tigers with a game-ending 17-7 run led by guards Juan Dixon and Drew Nicholas, coach Gary Williams finally could relax.

Maryland (14-3, 4-1 Atlantic Coast Conference) took over sole possession of second place in the ACC, increased its home record to 9-0 in its final season at Cole and righted itself in time to begin preparation for another ACC heavyweight match.

Clemson (11-8, 2-4) lost its seventh consecutive game to Maryland, but give the Tigers credit for serving the Terps with a splash of cold water, courtesy of some torrid shooting. Guards Tony Stockman and Edward Scott, who led Clemson with 22 and 20 points, respectively, took advantage of Maryland's lax perimeter defense by combining for 11 three-pointers.

As a team, the Tigers made 15 of 28 from beyond the arc, and held an 83-82 lead with 4:41 left.

NATIONAL CHAMPIONS

"It's all about winning. It doesn't matter how you get it," said senior Maryland guard Juan Dixon, who led the team with 23 points and set a school record for career three-pointers (189). He made the three-pointer that put Maryland in front to stay at 85-83.

"We came out pressing [on defense] and those guys got some open looks and made shots. They got some confidence, but we never stopped playing hard."

The Terps overcame an off shooting night by senior center Lonny Baxter, who missed seven of 12 free throws and a handful of close-range shots but still finished with 21 points.

In addition to Dixon, the Terps got a great night from sophomore forward Chris Wilcox, who used a career-high 28 minutes to counter Clemson almost single-handedly on the glass, finishing with 17 points and a game-high 14 rebounds. Junior backup guard Nicholas (14 points, six assists) took care of the rest by scoring all eight of his second-half points in the final three minutes.

"That game could have been lost very easily. That game was up there for the taking. I liked our heart down the stretch," said Williams, who watched Maryland surrender a 66-55 lead before kicking into a winning gear. "This is kind of exciting, to outscore the NBA when we play. If we can ever combine the way we play offense with good defense, we can be a very good team.

"I respected Clemson for [beating] Virginia, and I knew this would be tough after the Duke emotion," he added. "I'm totally concerned about our rebounding. Clemson was physical on the glass. We did some things tonight that weren't good defensively. We weren't aggressive early. But we did some good things down the stretch."

Maryland made nine of its last 11 free throws. Led by point guard Steve Blake (13 assists, two turnovers), the Terps took excellent care of the ball by committing a season-low six turnovers and exploited Clemson's 2-3 zone patiently with good penetration and ball movement on the perimeter. They also defended the wing much better in the second half by forcing a tiring Clemson team into 4-for-12 shooting from beyond the arc.

The Terps got their final burst of breathing room when Nicholas scored seven straight Maryland points—a three-pointer, two free throws and a short jumper—to give the Terps a 93-86 lead with 1:49 left. Dixon followed 39 seconds later by converting a three-point play to give Maryland a 96-88 advantage.

The Tigers aroused Maryland by playing rough on the inside. With 13:32 left in the first half, the teams nearly came to blows when Clemson forward Chris Hobbs (12 points, nine rebounds) tossed Maryland forward Tahj Holden to the floor and drew an intentional foul.

"I knew it was going to be a physical game, but we just couldn't back down from them," Wilcox said.

"When you collect talent and experience, you get yourself a whale of a ball club, which they certainly have," Clemson coach Larry Shyatt said of the Terps. "We chose to try to increase their three-point shot attempts and decrease their inside feeds [with the zone defense]. They have so many weapons."

"That game could have been lost very easily. That game was up there for the taking. I liked our heart down the stretch."

MARYLAND HEAD COACH
GARY WILLIAMS

DOUG KAPUSTIN, THE BALTIMORE SUN

January 20, 2002: Clemson vs. MARYLAND

	1st	2nd	Total
Clemson	48	42	90
MARYLAND	52	47	99

Clemson

Player	FG-FGA	3-PT FG-FGA	FT-FTA	O-D REB	A	BLK	S	TP
33 McKnight	6-11	3-4	4-7	3-3	4	1	0	19
43 Hobbs	4-9	0-0	4-7	4-5	1	0	1	12
21 Henderson	4-8	0-0	3-4	2-11	0	3	0	11
00 Stockman	8-16	6-13	0-0	2-2	2	0	0	22
10 Scott	7-17	5-8	1-2	1-6	8	0	0	20
03 Nagys	1-1	1-1	0-0	1-1	1	0	0	3
05 Ford	0-3	0-0	1-3	2-1	0	1	0	1
12 Babalola	0-1	0-1	0-0	1-1	0	1	0	0
14 Christie	0-1	0-1	0-0	1-0	0	0	0	0
35 Clifton	1-2	0-0	0-0	1-0	0	0	0	2

MARYLAND

Player	FG-FGA	3-PT FG-FGA	FT-FTA	O-D REB	A	BLK	S	TP
01 Mouton	4-8	4-6	2-2	0-4	3	0	0	14
54 Wilcox	7-15	0-0	3-5	7-7	1	1	1	17
35 Baxter	8-17	0-0	5-12	2-3	2	3	3	21
03 Dixon	8-18	4-10	3-3	2-0	2	0	3	23
25 Blake	1-5	1-5	0-0	2-2	13	0	1	3
10 Collins	0-0	0-0	0-0	0-0	0	0	0	0
12 Nicholas	4-7	2-5	4-5	0-4	6	1	0	14
33 Randle	1-1	0-0	1-3	1-2	0	1	0	3
45 Holden	0-1	0-0	4-6	0-0	0	2	0	4

DREW NICHOLAS

Call Terps' Nicholas Mr. Versatile

BY GARY LAMBRECHT

Drew Nicholas never expected to become a handyman in a basketball uniform. For the most versatile player in a Maryland Terrapins uniform, any job that keeps him on the floor is worth mastering. Playing time is that precious to Nicholas. The junior guard from New York's Long Island is making the most of his opportunities, and the Terps are a more dangerous team because of it.

On any given night, Nicholas, a long-armed 6 feet 3, comes off the bench to run the offense while giving point guard Steve Blake a rest. Or he spends much of his time at small forward, concentrating on playing defense and keeping a taller, aggressive swingman like Wake Forest's Josh Howard off the offensive boards. Or he fills in for shooting guard Juan Dixon and does what he likes best by firing away at the basket.

Typically, Nicholas spreads out his 20.4-minute contribution average by doing a little of everything and doing it well.

"Every night it's different, a different role each night," said Nicholas, who is averaging 6.9 points, 2.5 assists, 2.6 rebounds and only 1.2 turnovers. He's also shooting 50.5 percent from the field, including 39.1 percent from three-point range.

"It's been a process, a long process since I came in as a freshman. Coming from being labeled as a shooter to a point guard in my sophomore year. Now I'm playing three positions. Hopefully, it's helping me become a complete player. Hopefully, I won't have to play four positions next year."

Kidding aside, Nicholas has never looked more valuable to Maryland. All he did in the team's dramatic, come-from-behind 91-87 victory at Virginia was produce the two biggest shots heard in Charlottesville this year.

The Terps' comeback against Virginia from nine points down with 3:22 left was stamped with Nicholas' fingerprints. His 25-footer from the right wing cut Virginia's lead to 85-81 with 2:40 left, sending a pang of doubt into the Cavaliers and their boisterous fans. His 27-foot shot from the top of the key with 1:20 to go cut the lead to 87-86 and sent the Terps on a game-ending 8-0 run.

"It looked far," Nicholas said of his second shot, which completed the most significant six-point scoring line of the contest. "When I caught the ball, I just shot it. Even before the ball left my hand, I knew it was going in."

Nicholas then sealed the win when he blocked the game-tying three-point attempt in the closing seconds.

"He is as versatile as any player I've had," Williams said. "Handling the ball, playing big guys [on defense], running the point. He's like two guys coming off the bench. You can put him in different situations, and he handles it."

"He is as versatile as any player I've had."

MARYLAND HEAD COACH GARY WILLIAMS

DOUG KAPUSTIN, THE BALTIMORE SUN

Comeback Kids
Terrapins Rally Past Virginia, 91-87

by GARY LAMBRECHT

The Maryland Terrapins were brimming with confidence before coming to a place that has treated them harshly over the years, but the medicine they administered to a stunned Virginia team will not be forgotten anytime soon.

With a display of heart and grit befitting a team that envisions itself winning a national championship, No. 3 Maryland turned defeat into its most exhilarating victory of the season, erasing a seven-point deficit over the final three minutes and knocking off the No. 8 Cavaliers, 91-87, before a sellout crowd at University Hall. You want road warriors? The Terps fear no one. Not after beating a team that had taken down Maryland seven times in the past 10 meetings here, including an embarrassing, 21-point loss a year ago. Not after grinding through an evening when their best player found tough sledding against Virginia's best, only to have the Terps' bench rise up and steal the game in crunch time.

The Terps (17-3, 7-1) won their ninth game in 10 tries, matched their best eight-game start in the Atlantic Coast Conference ever under coach Gary Williams, kept pace with first-place Duke and concluded their first run through the conference schedule by essentially turning the ACC into a two-team race between Maryland and the Blue Devils.

"We've got a lot of heart. We've been through it. It's not like we haven't played big games on tough courts," said Williams, whose team closed the game with a 13-2 run. "That was a great game. We knew how to act down the stretch."

Depth is what got the Terps into their first Final Four last year, and depth carried the night in Charlottesville—beginning with all-purpose guard Drew Nicholas, who did not score for more than 37 minutes, then dropped two of the biggest three-pointers of his life on the Cavaliers (14-4, 4-4) to spark Maryland's amazing comeback.

"Those last three minutes, it still hasn't sunk in yet," said Nicholas, who wore the brightest, six-point scoring line of the night.

NATIONAL CHAMPIONS

After going scoreless in the first half, Maryland's bench of Nicholas, forward Tahj Holden and center Ryan Randle combined for 21 points in the second half.

With the Terps trailing 85-78, Nicholas threw some cold water on the delirious home crowd by hitting a 25-footer from the right wing to cut Virginia's lead to 85-81 with 2:26 left. After Maryland forward Byron Mouton and Virginia guard Roger Mason Jr. each made two free throws, Nicholas did it again from the top of the key, some 23 feet away.

That pulled Maryland to 87-86 with 1:19 left, and it changed the momentum dramatically. The Cavaliers, who seemingly were in control minutes earlier behind Mason's game-high 29 points, would never score again.

Maryland closed the deal by running off the game's last five points and making a series of great defensive stands. After Mason missed a go-ahead runner, Maryland center Lonny Baxter (14 points, 10 rebounds, four blocked shots) blocked Virginia center Travis Watson's follow-up. Watson then fumbled the ball out of bounds.

The Terps promptly converted, as senior guard Juan Dixon—held to only four second-half points by Mason at that point—hit a 10-foot, baseline runner to give the Terps an 88-87 lead with 32 seconds left. Virginia forward Chris Williams then missed a 15-footer. Holden grabbed the rebound, got fouled, and made two free throws to make it 90-87 with 13.7 seconds to go.

Nicholas then blocked Mason's game-tying, three-point attempt from the left corner. The Cavaliers retained possession, but freshman forward Elton Brown's three-point attempt missed. Mouton, who finished with a team-high and season-high 21 points and carried the Terps in the first half, then made one of two free throws to ice the contest.

That was the only free throw missed by Maryland, which made 25 of 26 from the line, the third-best single-game percentage in school history.

"I don't even know what to say about this team," said Dixon, who finished with 16 points and four assists, but watched others carry the action for a change.

"It was a great win. It does a lot for us, starting off 7-1 in the ACC," Nicholas said. "That's not too bad. [The Cavaliers] thought they had the victory, and the crowd was really into it. We remained mature. We were not going to let that game go."

The Cavaliers, behind Mason and Watson (19 points, game-high 12 rebounds), opened a 51-44 lead in the opening two minutes of the second half, then withstood five ties before losing the lead at 70-69 on Randle's shot with 7:48 to go. Virginia then went on a 14-4 run to take an 83-74 lead with 3:22 left.

"I was confident [down nine points with 3:22 left], but I was determined not to get blown out," Williams said. "I didn't want it to get to double digits."

Maryland got an additional spark during a timeout with 6:05 left, when Williams got into a brief shouting match with Virginia coach Pete Gillen, after Watson strayed too close to the Terps' huddle.

January 31, 2002: MARYLAND vs. Virginia

	1st	2nd	Total
MARYLAND	44	47	91
Virginia	46	41	87

MARYLAND

Player	FG-FGA	3-PT FG-FGA	FT-FTA	O-D REB	A	BLK	S	TP
01 Mouton	5-11	0-1	11-12	7-1	2	0	0	21
54 Wilcox	4-11	0-0	0-0	3-5	1	0	1	8
35 Baxter	6-10	0-0	2-2	3-7	0	4	1	14
03 Dixon	5-13	1-3	5-5	1-2	4	0	0	16
25 Blake	4-7	1-1	2-2	0-0	4	0	1	11
10 Collins	0-0	0-0	0-0	0-0	0	0	0	0
12 Nicholas	2-4	2-2	0-0	1-3	2	1	0	6
33 Randle	2-3	0-0	0-0	0-3	0	0	0	4
45 Holden	3-7	0-2	5-5	1-4	1	0	0	11

Virginia

Player	FG-FGA	3-PT FG-FGA	FT-FTA	O-D REB	A	BLK	S	TP
32 Mathias	1-4	0-0	1-2	3-2	0	1	0	3
33 Williams	2-8	0-1	9-13	1-3	5	1	0	13
35 Watson	9-16	0-0	1-4	10-2	1	1	1	19
10 Jenifer	2-5	0-0	0-0	0-3	3	0	1	4
21 Mason	8-21	5-11	8-8	0-2	5	0	3	29
24 Harper	1-1	1-1	4-4	0-3	2	0	0	7
31 Hall	0-2	0-2	0-0	1-0	0	0	0	0
34 Clark	1-1	0-0	0-0	0-0	0	2	1	2
42 Brown	4-8	2-4	0-0	0-2	1	0	0	10

STEVE HELBER, AP/WIDE WORLD PHOTOS

Rare Rout Shakes Duke to Its Core

Usually Dominant Devils Get 'Flustered,' Suffer Most One-Sided Loss in Four Years

by DON MARKUS

They looked like imposters in black and blue, a team that resembled Duke in name and face but certainly not in execution and intensity. That's what Maryland did to the Blue Devils at Cole Field House. That's what top-ranked Duke did to itself.

Was that really Jason Williams, one of the favorites for national Player of the Year, missing 16 of 22 shots and making six turnovers during Duke's 87-73 loss to the No. 3 Terrapins? Was that really Mike Dunleavy, an All-Atlantic Coast Conference candidate himself, missing nine of 14 shots and being dominated inside by Maryland's Chris Wilcox? Having won 11 straight games by an average of 23 points since their only previous loss of the season last month at Florida State, having won by 37 on Thursday night at home over No. 24 North Carolina State, Duke found itself in a strange place—behind by as many as 25 points in the second half.

"We weren't that good, but Maryland had a lot to do with it," said Duke coach Mike Krzyzewski. " . . . We really rushed things early

in the game. We got flustered. You can get that way when the other team isn't playing that well, but Maryland was playing well."

It was Duke's most one-sided loss since a 15-point defeat to North Carolina in the 1998 ACC tournament final, when the Blue Devils were ranked first and the Tar Heels fourth. The Blue Devils shot a season-low 36 percent (27-for-75) from the field, made just seven of 33 three-point attempts and committed 18 turnovers.

Oh, and did we mention that they missed eight of their first nine free throws in a 12-for-24 afternoon?

"They played great defense, they pressured a lot of shots; Lonny Baxter did a great job inside blocking shots and helping," said Williams, who finished with 17 points, six turnovers and four assists. "A lot of teams play me physically. Maryland did a great job of always knowing where I was as soon as I caught the ball."

DOUG KAPUSTIN, THE BALTIMORE SUN

NATIONAL CHAMPIONS

Said Dunleavy, "Jason wasn't hitting the shots he normally does, but a lot of that had to do with the defense [Steve] Blake played on him."

Williams was involved in what turned out to be a key play in helping Maryland reclaim the momentum it had for most of the first half. Having cut a 14-point deficit in half, Williams was trying to set the offense for the final play. He looked back at Krzyzewski for a play to call, and Blake stripped the ball and scored.

"He was trying to call a play, and I couldn't hear what he was saying " Williams said. "I looked at him again because everyone was telling me. And he [Blake] stole the ball. He made a good play."

Things only got worse in the second half for the Blue Devils. They scored twice in the first nine possessions and three times in the first seven minutes as their deficit grew to 17. They found themselves down by as many as 25 on three occasions in the second half.

While the Maryland fans and even a few of the players were mindful of what happened last season against Duke—first losing in overtime at home after blowing a 10-point lead in the final 54 seconds of regulation, then watching a 22-point lead in the first half of their NCAA

tournament semifinal disappear—the Blue Devils realized it wasn't happening again.

"We knew it would be pretty difficult to come back, as well as they were playing," Dunleavy said.

Duke made its last run after scoring nine straight points to cut its deficit to 69-54 on a three-point play by freshman guard Daniel Ewing with 7:42 to play. And when the Blue Devils got within 81-70 with a little over two minutes left, the fans and Wilcox got nervous.

"I said to myself, 'This isn't happening again,'" Wilcox recalled later.

It didn't, mostly because of the mistakes Duke made earlier.

"We didn't do the things we needed to do to get back in the game," said Duke assistant coach Steve Wojciechowski.

The defeat puts the Blue Devils in a precarious position in terms of winning their sixth straight ACC regular-season championship. At 11-2, they trail Maryland (11-1) and must still play at Wake Forest and Virginia. It also means the ACC tournament will likely determine the top seed in the East region of the NCAA tournament.

> **"A lot of teams play me physically. Maryland did a great job of always knowing where I was as soon as I caught the ball."**
>
> DUKE GUARD JASON WILLIAMS

DOUG KAPUSTIN, THE BALTIMORE SUN

February 17, 2002: Duke vs. MARYLAND

	1st	2nd	Total
Duke	29	44	73
MARYLAND	38	49	87

Duke

Player	FG-FGA	3-PT FG-FGA	FT-FTA	O-D REB	A	BLK	S	TP
30 Jones	1-8	0-1	3-4	2-3	2	1	0	5
34 Dunleavy	5-14	3-10	2-6	3-8	0	0	1	15
04 Boozer	8-10	0-0	3-5	6-6	3	1	0	19
21 Duhon	3-12	1-7	0-0	1-1	7	0	0	7
22 Williams	6-22	2-12	3-6	3-3	4	0	3	17
03 Horvath	1-1	0-0	0-0	1-1	0	2	0	2
05 Ewing	3-8	1-3	1-3	1-2	1	0	1	8

MARYLAND

Player	FG-FGA	3-PT FG-FGA	FT-FTA	O-D REB	A	BLK	S	TP
01 Mouton	7-14	0-2	1-2	1-8	3	0	1	15
54 Wilcox	8-16	0-0	7-9	6-5	3	0	2	23
35 Baxter	3-8	0-0	5-6	0-10	0	4	0	11
03 Dixon	8-14	1-2	0-0	0-2	0	0	2	17
25 Blake	3-8	0-3	2-3	0-6	13	1	3	8
12 Nicholas	1-3	1-2	2-2	0-2	3	0	0	5
33 Randle	1-3	0-0	0-0	1-0	0	0	1	2
45 Holden	1-2	0-0	4-4	2-0	0	0	0	6

NATIONAL CHAMPIONS

DOUG KAPUSTIN, THE BALTIMORE SUN

GARY WILLIAMS

In a Zone, Williams Makes All Right Moves

by MIKE PRESTON

Gary Williams can coach. In successive games, he has beaten two of college basketball's best in Kentucky's Tubby Smith and Connecticut's Jim Calhoun. That's impressive.

So was the job Williams did in directing Maryland to a thrilling 90-82 victory against Connecticut in the East Regional championship game at the Carrier Dome.

His moves and strategies might get lost in the euphoria of the victory over Connecticut, which has to be an ESPN Instant Classic candidate because of its relentless pace, great individual efforts and back-and-forth nature, which included 24 lead changes and 21 ties. But Williams was at his best against one of the best.

On a night when his starting point guard was terrible except at crunch time, when three starters were in foul trouble midway through the second half and Maryland could have lost its composure late in the game, Williams pushed all the right buttons.

He went to a zone defense that caused the Huskies problems late in the first half, and again late in the second half. He was daring by re-inserting Dixon and other starters despite foul trouble. And he stayed with the basic strategy that got him here by continuing to pound the ball inside for most of the game.

Beautiful.

I'm giving Williams The Genius label for a day. I can't give it to him for longer than that because the true Genius in the area (his initials are BB and he works for the Ravens) might get offended. But Williams wouldn't care, anyway, because he doesn't read newspapers.

He leaves that job to his assistants, who were a little irritated that some Baltimore and Washington newspapers gave Smith and Calhoun the edge over Williams in the coaching matchups.

How dare they?

But that he-can't-coach rap seems to have followed Williams to American University, Boston College, Ohio State and Maryland even though he has a 479-271 record in 24 years.

Bob Wade wishes he could have coached like that.

If Williams has had one major problem over the years, it's not going to his bench because he often gets caught up in the emotion of games. But that's not true anymore, especially after the Connecticut win.

Maryland won two games, the one on the court and the one between Williams and Calhoun.

The Huskies were quicker than Maryland and wanted to spread out the Terps to isolate them one-on-one. But with about seven minutes left in the first half, Williams went to a 3-2 zone, which he likes about as much as he likes Duke.

That zone, however, helped force three turnovers before the half, and Maryland outscored the Huskies 16-10 for a 44-37 halftime lead.

Trailing by three points, Maryland went back to the zone with 4:49 remaining in the game and outscored the Huskies 18-7 for the victory. The Terps were well prepared, knowing where the shooters would be until Calhoun made changes late in the game.

"I thought if we got the game spread that they could not play with us due to our quickness," Calhoun said. "The game actually came to that, but Gary made a nice move and went to primarily a zone."

The zone was somewhat of a new wrinkle, but pounding the ball inside to center Lonny Baxter for 29 points wasn't. Maybe that doesn't sound like a big deal, but the so-called geniuses in sports often abandon what works well. They start believing in those genius labels.

But not Williams. When Huskies forward Caron Butler was sent to the bench along with center Emeka Okafor for his second foul with 5:15 left in the first half, Williams kept going to Baxter, who scored eight points in the last 3:25.

When Okafor committed his third foul a minute into the second half, the Terps went to Baxter for seven points within the next two minutes. "That's what Lonny Baxter has given us for three-plus years," Williams said.

Williams had to work more combinations than a safe cracker in the second half. Forward Chris Wilcox committed his third foul with 16:10 left in the game. Point guard Steve Blake had his third about four minutes

later, and Dixon was whistled for his third with 9:37 left.

No one fouled out.

"If you look at what he has done thoughtout his coaching career at American University, Ohio State and Maryland, it's pretty unbelievable," said Terps assistant coach David Dickerson. "In my estimation, he is one of the best coaches out there. Look at what he did tonight in finding all those combinations. He made all the right decisions. That's why he is a great coach."

LLOYD FOX, THE BALTIMORE SUN

Wake Gives UM Time to Win, 90-89

With 1.3 Seconds Left, Demon Deacons Call One Timeout Too Many

by GARY LAMBRECHT

Forty minutes of tense, classic basketball boiled down to one free throw and one huge mistake at Cole Field House, where the Maryland Terrapins finally were pushed to the brink of defeat.

But the No. 2 Maryland men, who spent most of the final 28 minutes trailing No. 20 Wake Forest, protected their first-place lead in the Atlantic Coast Conference because the Terps refused to blink while escaping with a 90-89 victory before a sellout crowd. "I don't think anybody needs the stress and strain of a one-point game like this, but you'd rather learn from winning than learn from losing," said Maryland forward Tahj Holden. "This was a good day to learn."

It was an excruciating finish for the Demon Deacons, who, after putting the first major scare into Maryland (23-3, 13-1 ACC) in its house this season, probably still are wondering how they could have let a chance to force overtime slip away.

And Wake Forest small forward Josh Howard, who was spectacular in the second half after

teammate Craig Dawson lit up the place with his three-point shooting and put the Terps in a 56-46 halftime hole, probably still is wondering how he could have committed such an error in judgment.

With 1.3 seconds left and the score tied 89-89, Maryland got a gift courtesy of Howard. After grabbing a rebound of a missed 8-foot jumper by Terps guard Juan Dixon, Howard signaled for a timeout that Wake Forest did not have. That resulted in a technical foul, which put Dixon on the foul line and allowed him to deliver the winning point.

After Dixon's missed second foul shot, Wake Forest saw its upset bid fail as guard Broderick Hicks tossed up a long air ball at the buzzer.

This was not the Wake Forest team Maryland has come to own in recent years. This was not the Wake Forest team that rolled over against Duke last week and lost by 29 at home.

This group tore through Maryland's defensive pressure with 62.9 percent shooting in the first half, absorbed a 13-4 Maryland run to begin

---

the second half that cut the Wake lead to 60-59 with 16:54 left, then dug in with the Terps for a tight stretch run. The Demon Deacons (18-10, 8-6) withstood three ties and never led by more than five before they lost their advantage.

The Terps, after taking a 34-33 lead with 8:26 left in the first half, did not take the lead again until a free throw by Byron Mouton gave them an 86-85 edge with 1:51 to go. And it all came down to a miscue by Howard, who simply failed to hear the instructions of Wake Forest coach Skip Prosser.

"I wasn't paying attention in the huddle. I can make up a million excuses, but I just let down my team," said Howard, who had missed the past two weeks with a high ankle sprain and came off the bench to score 18 points and grab a game-high 15 rebounds. Howard also scored the put-back that tied the score with 10.2 seconds left.

"[Howard] allowed us to get two free throws. I'm going to feel sorry for him. He's a great player, and he played well," said Dixon, who finished with 20 points and six rebounds, despite shooting 6-for-16. "That's something that should have been done in the huddle. It's a bogus play, but next time somebody should inform him that they don't have any timeouts left."

During a season in which they have won every which way, the Terps hit another new note in their next-to-last show at Cole, while winning their 10th straight game, maintaining a one-game lead on Duke in the ACC regular-season title race and becoming the first Maryland team to win 23 of its first 26.

"We've been down before at the half, but that game obviously stayed tight the whole way.

That's a great win for us," said Maryland coach Gary Williams, whose team had never trailed at home at the half this season and had beaten six other conference opponents there by an average of 19 before Wake.

"A lot of teams wouldn't win that game, but we found a way to win it. I don't care if it's pretty. I don't care what happened. We won the game."

Maryland was a mess defensively in the early going, as the Demon Deacons beat the press and kept feeding Dawson, who entered the game as the league's top three-point shooter. Dawson scored 22 first-half points, bolstered by 6-for-7 shooting from beyond the three-point arc.

Senior center Darius Songaila also gave the Demon Deacons inspired play with 20 points, six rebounds and six assists.

But in the second half, the Terps, who had not given up that many points before the break this season, dropped back into their half-court defense, took Dawson out of the action and began to attack Wake Forest's matchup zone defense.

Wake Forest shot 33.3 percent in the second half, and went into a 2-for-9 drought over the final 5:25. After being carried by senior center Lonny Baxter, who scored 19 of his team-high 25 in the first half, the cavalry arrived for the Terps.

Sophomore forward Chris Wilcox scored 11 of his 13 and grabbed all nine of his rebounds in the second half. Junior point guard Steve Blake finished with eight points and 13 assists, including 11 assists and one turnover in the second half.

Wilcox scored seven of Maryland's last 13 points, including a free throw that put Maryland in front 87-85 and a leaner over Songaila that gave the Terps a 89-87 lead with 25 seconds left. Howard then tied the score on a put-back, was fouled by Wilcox on the play, missed the ensuing foul shot, then grabbed his biggest rebound of the game and followed with his biggest mistake.

"It was a little close, but it's fun to be part of a team that knows how to win and how to finish games," Blake said. "A little luck can never hurt. But we put ourselves in position to get that help."

February 24, 2002: Wake Forest vs. MARYLAND

	1st	2nd	Total
Wake Forest	56	33	89
MARYLAND	46	44	90

Wake Forest

Player	FG-FGA	3-PT FG-FGA	FT-FTA	O-D REB	A	BLK	S	TP
33 Lepore	3-6	2-5	0-0	0-1	0	0	1	8
34 Scott	1-2	0-0	2-2	1-4	0	0	0	4
25 Songaila	7-11	0-0	6-6	2-4	6	0	1	20
04 Downey	2-5	0-2	0-0	1-1	4	0	2	4
42 Dawson	10-13	7-9	0-1	0-2	1	0	1	27
03 Hicks	1-10	0-4	0-1	0-2	3	0	1	2
05 Howard	8-16	0-5	2-5	4-11	1	1	2	18
13 Danelius	2-8	0-0	2-2	3-1	0	0	1	6

MARYLAND

Player	FG-FGA	3-PT FG-FGA	FT-FTA	O-D REB	A	BLK	S	TP
01 Mouton	6-12	2-6	5-7	1-2	2	0	0	19
54 Wilcox	6-7	0-0	1-4	2-7	2	1	1	13
35 Baxter	11-13	0-0	3-5	1-7	1	3	2	25
03 Dixon	6-16	2-9	6-7	1-5	3	0	1	20
25 Blake	4-11	0-5	0-0	1-1	13	1	1	8
12 Nicholas	0-3	0-3	0-0	0-1	4	0	0	0
33 Randle	1-1	0-0	0-0	0-1	1	0	0	2
45 Holden	1-1	1-1	0-0	2-3	1	0	1	3

NATIONAL CHAMPIONS

KENNETH K. LAM, THE BALTIMORE SUN

Terps Slam Door Shut
UM Routs Virginia, Caps Perfect Ending

by GARY LAMBECHT

There was no way the Maryland Terrapins were going to leave their fans with a tarnished memory. Not on this night. Not in this house.

The second-ranked Terps completed the greatest regular season in school history and kissed their cherished home court goodbye in style, by taking control of Virginia early and running the Cavaliers out of College Park, 112-92, before the final sellout crowd at Cole Field House.

Virginia came to Maryland's floor following a huge upset win over Duke that gave the slumping Cavaliers renewed momentum as they angled for an NCAA tournament berth. But Virginia hit the same wall that has slammed so many other opponents here this season.

The Terps (25-3, 15-1), who won their 12th consecutive game while completing their first unbeaten season at home since 1995—and only the fourth in the 47-year history of Cole—won as they have all year. They jabbed effectively early, then delivered a knockout blow later.

With an 18-4 run to open the second half, the Terps turned a 43-36 halftime lead into a 61-40 advantage with 15:15 left. Maryland would stretch the lead to 24 points, as the outcome was never in doubt.

"We have a good team. It's not one guy. It's a group of people who have decided to be the best they can be this year," Terps coach Gary Williams said. "I think this team has done as good a job as any I've had at taking care of each game as it comes. I'm proud of them."

Everybody joined the party, as six players scored in double figures, punctuating a night when the Terps softened up Virginia's zone defense early with outside shooting and offensive rebounding, then ate up Virginia's man-to-man with its vaunted front line in the second half.

Three players hit the 20-point mark for Maryland. Guard Juan Dixon and center Lonny Baxter, the seniors who have been the spine of this team since October, put forth memorable stamps on Senior Night. Dixon scored 17 of his team-high 23 points in the second half. Baxter finished with 20 points and

KARL MERTON FERRON, THE BALTIMORE SUN

NATIONAL CHAMPIONS

eight rebounds, including 13 points after halftime.

The rest of the second half, which featured 72.7 percent shooting by Maryland, belonged to sophomore forward Chris Wilcox. He manhandled Virginia forwards Chris Williams and J.C. Mathis with 21 points and 11 rebounds. Wilcox had 16 points and seven rebounds in the second half.

Junior point guard Steve Blake overcame early foul trouble and a subpar first half by finishing with a double-double. Blake had 15 points and 10 assists. Senior forward Byron Mouton added 11 points, five assists and four rebounds.

Senior forward Chris Williams led Virginia (17-10, 7-9) with a career-high 28 points. Center Travis Watson finished with 20 points.

Nearly all of the 14,500 who attended stayed to watch a series of post-game ceremonies, which ended with Maryland cutting down the nets to celebrate its first regular-season Atlantic Coast Conference championship since 1980. Maryland heads into this week's ACC tournament as the top seed, and will open on Friday against the winner of Thursday night's Clemson-Florida State play-in game.

The Cavaliers started with some fire. They were determined to contain Dixon, and they swarmed enough out of their 2-3 matchup zone defense to hold him scoreless and limit him to five shots through the game's first 13 minutes.

But even with Dixon's lack of early production, and despite Blake getting into early foul trouble, the Cavaliers could not keep Wilcox or Baxter off the offensive glass, could not keep Mouton from beating them to loose balls, could not keep the Terps from finding other answers to erase a 19-14 deficit.

Drew Nicholas started a 9-2 run that turned the game in Maryland's favor by sinking a three-pointer from the right wing. A Baxter layup off a Wilcox lob then tied the score at 19. After Wilcox converted a free throw following a Virginia turnover, Mouton drove the baseline, made a layup, then converted a three-point play to give the Terps a 23-19 lead with 9:12 left in the half.

Virginia scored three points to calm the crowd temporarily, but the Terps got the heat rising again with a 16-2 run that put the Cavaliers in a 39-24 hole with 3:55 to go.

Dixon, using a great baseline screen from Tahj Holden—who started the run by hitting a 17-footer—broke his scoreless drought with a backdoor layup off a Mouton assist with 6:48 left, extending Maryland's lead to 28-22. After a runner by Virginia point guard Keith Jenifer (Towson Catholic) cut the lead to four, the Terps scored the next 11 points.

Nicholas started it with a three-pointer from the top of the key. Mouton and Dixon took over from there. Mouton converted two free throws. After Ryan Randle blocked a shot by Jenifer, Dixon nailed a 15-foot baseline jumper, then made two free throws after being intentionally fouled by Jenifer.

Mouton finished the run with typical hustle. First, he kept a loose ball alive after a missed shot by Maryland. Then, he worked himself in the open, where he hit a 12-footer to complete the run.

Virginia finally regained some momentum with a 12-4 run to close the half. Chris Williams accounted for eight points, including a 23-footer at the buzzer to trim Maryland's halftime lead to 43-36.

LLOYD FOX, THE BALTIMORE SUN

March 3, 2002: Virginia vs. MARYLAND

	1st	2nd	Total
Virginia	36	56	92
MARYLAND	43	69	112

Virginia

Player	FG-FGA	3-PT FG-FGA	FT-FTA	O-D REB	A	BLK	S	TP
31 Hall	2-5	1-2	2-2	1-3	2	0	1	7
33 Williams	10-18	3-6	5-5	5-2	7	0	3	28
35 Watson	8-15	1-4	3-6	0-3	2	2	0	20
10 Jenifer	1-3	0-0	2-2	1-0	1	0	1	4
21 Mason	5-11	2-7	3-3	0-2	4	0	0	15
05 Dowling	0-0	0-0	0-0	0-0	0	0	0	0
12 Gladstone	0-0	0-0	0-0	0-0	0	0	0	0
24 Harper	2-6	1-3	2-2	1-2	1	1	0	7
30 Rogers	0-0	0-0	0-0	0-0	1	0	1	0
32 Mathis	0-2	0-0	0-0	0-0	0	0	0	0
34 Clark	4-4	0-0	1-2	3-1	0	1	0	9
42 Brown	0-0	0-0	2-3	1-0	0	0	0	2

MARYLAND

Player	FG-FGA	3-PT FG-FGA	FT-FTA	O-D REB	A	BLK	S	TP
01 Mouton	4-8	0-2	3-3	3-1	5	1	1	11
35 Baxter	8-10	0-0	4-5	2-6	0	3	2	20
54 Wilcox	8-9	0-0	5-6	5-6	4	1	1	21
03 Dixon	9-19	1-5	4-4	1-2	2	0	0	23
25 Blake	4-7	3-4	4-6	0-0	10	1	0	15
04 Badu	1-1	0-0	0-0	0-1	1	0	0	2
05 McCall	0-0	0-0	0-0	0-0	0	0	0	0
10 Collins	1-1	1-1	1-2	0-1	0	0	0	4
12 Nicholas	2-4	2-2	4-4	0-1	3	0	0	10
21 Grinnon	0-0	0-0	0-0	0-0	0	0	0	0
33 Randle	2-4	0-0	0-0	1-2	0	2	0	4
45 Holden	1-2	0-0	0-0	0-2	0	0	0	2

NATIONAL CHAMPIONS

COLE FIELDHOUSE

Cole History Packed with Fun, Games

by PAUL MCMULLEN

It was the launching pad for Len Bias and Steve Francis, the floor where John Lucas and Juan Dixon pulled up off the dribble, and where Lefty Driesell and Gary Williams stomped their feet and ruined perfectly good sport coats.

It's where legends like Adolph Rupp, Kareem Abdul-Jabbar and Michael Jordan lost. Not bad for a joint that opened as a white elephant.

It's fitting that the last opponent in the symmetrical hangar will be the same as the first. Maryland was trying to bury its cow college image when the Terps beat Virginia, 67-55, on Dec. 2, 1955. Then the second-largest arena in the East, after an earlier version of Madison Square Garden, Cole compiled a legacy as distinctive as that of any college court.

The last NCAA men's basketball championship decided on a campus came at Cole. It's the only on-campus arena to be the host of two NCAA finals, and the first carried great sociological weight. It never housed a No. 1 men's team, but top-ranked squads fell there a record seven times, and hype over the closing coincides with what might be Maryland's best team ever. Dixon and company can complete a fourth perfect season at Cole, where the Terps are 485-151.

Fans got an assist in plenty of those wins. There was the night in 1971 when a tentative South Carolina team was undone; the environment helped unranked Terps teams knock off No. 1 three times. Better Maryland squads benefited as well. Just two weeks ago, Duke's Jason Williams was bedeviled by the decibel level and Steve Blake. Scalpers got $1,000 for that showdown. With dozens of former Terps greats making a sentimental last call, tickets for the final night might fetch more.

Next autumn Williams will move his budding dynasty a couple of hundred yards north into the Comcast Center, which will cost more than $107 million. Cole's predecessor was built during the Great Depression, when the bill for Ritchie Coliseum was $176,000. The Student Activities Building—it wasn't named for Board of Regents Chairman William P. Cole until 1956—cost $3.2 million, and critics questioned every penny.

Running out of the tunnel and into an adoring arena is priceless. Dixon will be the last captain to lead the Terps onto the floor. Coach Bud Millikan gave that honor in 1955 to another Baltimorean, John Sandbower.

He had played at cramped Ritchie, on a floor so close to the stands that players were "three feet from falling into a coed's lap, if you were lucky." But the setting for Sandbower's senior year was far grander.

"We were pretty excited with the idea of playing in a palace, but there was very little hoopla or buildup to the opening," said Sandbower, now a local attorney. "The place looked as big as Texas when I came running out of that tunnel. It looked like the whole university was there."

The NCAA tournament stopped at Cole eight times from 1962 to '70. CBS analyst Billy Packer started for Wake Forest when it beat St. Joseph's in Cole's first NCAA tournament game. Towson native Billy Jones broke the ACC color barrier in 1965-66 when he suited up for the Terps. That same season, all-white Kentucky, coached by Rupp, lost the NCAA final at Cole to Texas Western, which used seven players, all African-Americans.

The finals of the state high school boys tournament have been a fixture at Cole since 1956, but its biggest prep games involved DeMatha.

Morgan Wootten's Stags played Power Memorial and Lew Alcindor—who later changed his name to Abdul-Jabbar —in 1964 and '65 at Cole. The latter game sold out three weeks in advance, and produced Abdul-Jabbar's only high school loss. Bragging rights in Washington are now settled at MCI Center, but the best city title game ever came at Cole in 1991, when DeMatha and Duane Simpkins roared back and beat D.C.'s Dunbar and Johnny Rhodes.

Byrd Stadium got Queen Elizabeth; Cole, the king of rock 'n' roll. On two nights in September 1974, Elvis Presley played Cole. From the swing of Benny Goodman to the rock of Bruce Springsteen and Bob Dylan, a broad spectrum of musical performances was staged at Cole, but never in the summer. It lacks air conditioning.

Ice storms often accompanied the CYO Games, which kicked off the East Coast indoor track and field circuit on the second Friday night in January from the late 1960s into the

'80s. Four months before Steve Prefontaine died in an alcohol-related accident, America's best distance talent was outdueled by Marty Liquori in a memorable 1975 mile.

Pingpong diplomacy stopped by in 1972, when the United States played host to China in table tennis. Billie Jean King played tennis and gymnast Olga Korbut tumbled in Cole. It played host to five NCAA wrestling tournaments, and one very absurd challenge match between two very tall men. The late Owen Brown, a forward for the Terps in the early 1970s, got hustled on the mats one day by Driesell, who pinned him twice.

"I went to Granby High in Norfolk," Driesell said last week of the home of the "Granby Roll," a basic wrestling move. "Players would get to bragging, and I would tell them I'd take bottom to start. I knew that Granby Roll. Pinned one of my players just last year. Probably reinjured my neck."

Vibrant in its old age, Cole was a quiet child, polite to visitors until its 15th winter. Like a teen-ager that can't control its hormones or voice, Maryland shouted its way onto the basketball scene in 1969, when Driesell was hired a few days after his Davidson team lost a heartbreaker to North Carolina in the East Regional final—at Cole.

"Lefty Driesell and Cole Field House are synonymous," former athletic director Jim Kehoe said of basketball's status at Maryland. "If it hadn't been for Lefty, the packed houses and the need for a new arena, none of this would have happened."

Driesell fiddled with one of Cole's crucial measurements. The sole concourse that fans descend from narrows to barely 10 feet, but it's 30 feet from sideline to the cement bowl that holds 12,230 permanent seats. Millikan coached in that sterile environment, but Driesell bridged that gap by demanding risers and folding chairs around the floor.

The added seats increased the listed capacity to 14,500. That has been exceeded on several occasions. Everyone from prep prospects to pachyderms drew applause during the Driesell era as the Terps tried promotions of all kinds.

"On Circus Night, we couldn't get an elephant out of the tunnel and it delayed the start of the second half," said Virginia state Sen. Russ Potts, who promoted Maryland basketball and football in the 1970s. "Kehoe was livid. I told him, 'The elephant won't listen to me, you talk to him.' I think that was the last Circus Night."

A win over Duke in Driesell's first season led to the singing of "Amen," which became to Maryland victories what Red Auerbach's cigar was to Boston Celtics titles. North Carolina coach Dean Smith once told his players at the half that he would serenade them with the spiritual if they came back and won. The Heels did.

Driesell's second season brought a monumental 31-30 win over No. 2 South Carolina. Their first meeting ended in a blowout and brawl in Columbia, the Terps losing both. After weeks of verbal jousting between Driesell and counterpart Frank McGuire, the Gamecocks came to Cole and were "protected" by the Maryland Medieval Mercenary Militia, a group of students playing dress-up. After an overtime victory, students tried to topple the baskets.

McGuire and South Carolina left the ACC, but other villains arrived.

Smith, the winningest coach in college basketball history, punched his ticket to three Final Fours and went 30-12 at Cole. He notched more wins there than Frank Fellows and Bob Wade, who preceded and followed Driesell.

Duke coach Mike Krzyzewski went 15-1 at Cole from 1985 to 2001, the last being maybe the most galling Terps defeat there, as the team blew a 10-point lead in the last 54 seconds.

Its bookend came in 1973, in the first made-for-TV college game on Super Bowl Sunday. David Thompson's first visit to Cole quieted the crowd, as the best player in ACC history—sorry MJ and Ralph Sampson—leaped over a textbook box-out by Bob Bodell for the winning put-back.

Ernie Graham often took a back seat to Albert King, but the Baltimorean had a performance for the ages in 1979, when he dropped 44 points on N.C. State. His school record would be 50 if there had been a three-point line.

Dixon is chasing Bias' school scoring record, but no one got more at Cole than Adrian Branch, who dropped in 1,028 points from 1982 to '85. Twenty-nine came in a deliberate overtime win over Virginia in February 1992.

A string of sellouts and an 85-game nonconference home-court streak will carry over to Comcast, but Cole was less than half full in December 1989, when Williams' first team was beaten by Coppin State. Eagles players were met with incredulity when they claimed they beat Maryland; disbelief engulfed Cole, too.

"There weren't a lot of people here who had great dreams," Williams said. "We had to create dreams."

Walt Williams warmed Cole through some hard winters, and Maryland became known to the NCAA as a participant rather than a host when Keith Booth and Joe Smith arrived in 1993. The third member of that recruiting class was Matt Kovarik, a current assistant who joined Reggie Jackson (1979-82) as the only Terps players to experience two wins over No. 1 at Cole. Both of Kovarik's, in 1995 and '98, came against North Carolina.

"It is absolutely amazing how this has all worked out," said Gary Williams, whose legacy includes a school record 8-for-8 shooting performance in December 1966, during his senior season with the Terps.

Cole has produced three Final Four teams for women's coach Chris Weller, 11 men's All-Americans from Tom McMillen through Dixon and a million memories.

The squad that opened Cole and the 1958 NCAA team will be honored at halftime of the final game. The post-game will include a "ball-passing" ceremony linking former Terps and the holdovers who will move into Comcast.

"I'm really, really sad," said former Terps guard Mo Howard. "The new place is going to be state-of-the-art. That's well and good, but Cole is always going to be my home court."

LLOYD FOX, THE BALTIMORE SUN

> "The new place is going to be state-of-the-art. ... but Cole is always going to be my home court."
> FORMER TERPS GUARD MO HOWARD

107

Terps Tame 'Noles, 85-59

Up 1 with 15:10 left, UM Goes on 21-0 Run to Snap Out of Funk

by GARY LAMBRECHT

The Maryland Terrapins hardly produced a stellar, wire-to-wire effort as they opened the 49th annual Atlantic Coast Conference tournament, but the top-seeded, second-ranked Terps only needed six minutes to remind Florida State that they were in charge.

Maryland won its 13th consecutive game and moved on to its eighth straight ACC tournament semifinal by pounding the eighth-seeded Seminoles, 85-59, before 23,895 at Charlotte Coliseum. The only surprise to emerge from the rout, which puts Maryland (26-3) up against North Carolina State, was how much sweat the Terps had to break to dispose of Florida State.

After an uneven first half in which they pretty much controlled the Seminoles while taking a 40-28 lead, the Terps broke form by getting off to a lazy, second-half start, while Florida State began the half with a 13-2 run to shave Maryland's lead to 42-41 with 15:10 left.

At that point, Seminoles guard Monte Cummings was abusing Maryland's Juan Dixon, and the Seminoles had turned four Maryland turnovers into points. At that point, Maryland

coach Gary Williams had burned two quick timeouts, and Williams chose to leave the Maryland huddle during an ensuing television timeout, leaving senior forward Byron Mouton to address his teammates with some choice words.

And right after that point, the Terps brought reality crashing down on the Seminoles with a furious, 21-0 run that put Maryland firmly in front, 63-41, with 9:13 to go.

From there, Maryland gradually emptied its bench against a tired opponent. The Seminoles (12-17), whose coach, Steve Robinson, most likely has run his last game in Tallahassee, were playing only 14 hours after winning an overtime, play-in game against Clemson, 91-84.

"We weren't mentally tough enough for 20 minutes in the first half. Then, the first four minutes [of the second half] were a nightmare. Then, we picked it up," said Williams, who took a rare walk away from his huddle before watching the Terps take out the Seminoles.

"I had nothing good to say, so I got out of there," he added. "I had made my point during

---

NATIONAL CHAMPIONS

the previous timeout. I would have burned another one [if not for TV]. The way that thing was going we had to get it stopped somehow. I was upset, no doubt. These guys have worked too hard, too long."

That left the motivational speaking duties to Mouton, one of Maryland's three seniors.

"I wanted to get them mad and frustrated," said Mouton, who scored 14 of his 18 points in the first half, added seven rebounds and also drew the team's first technical foul of the season, in the first half. "I wanted them to go out there and be aggressive. I wanted them to take it out on Florida State. The next thing you know, we were up by 18 or 19 points."

The next thing you knew, the Terps started acting like themselves again, and so did Florida State, which went 12 possessions without a point during its collapse and ended the game with 19 turnovers, only seven assists and shot just 30 percent from the field.

The next thing you knew, Maryland started creating fast-break points out of its full-court pressure and started shredding Florida State's 2-3 zone with great ball movement. And Dixon, after surrendering 10 straight Florida State points to Cummings to start the second half, answered like an All-America player should by scoring nine of his game-high 20 points after that pivotal timeout.

Point guard Steve Blake, who gave the Terps a little bit of everything with 10 points, seven assists, five rebounds and five steals, started the big run with a three-pointer from the right wing, giving Maryland a 45-41 lead with 14:42 left. At the 12:57 mark, Dixon turned a great feed from Blake into a three-pointer, making it 52-41.

Backup guard Drew Nicholas followed with a three-point play. Blake then stole an in-bounds pass and fed Dixon, who nailed a 15-foot, baseline jumper. Another Blake steal led to a layup by center Lonny Baxter (10 points, three rebounds, three steals, two blocks). A hook shot by backup center Ryan Randle and a tip-in by backup forward Tahj Holden finished the run.

"When we got it to about 49-41, I looked at a couple of their guys and it was like, 'Damn, we had our chance. This might be it,'" Dixon said. "Florida State gave us their best effort. They had an emotional game last night, and we knew they were going to come out ready to play."

Cummings led the Seminoles with 19 points. Center Nigel Dixon had 13 points, 12 rebounds and eight turnovers. Senior point guard Delvon Arrington finished his collegiate career on a down note by scoring nine points on 3-for-13 shooting, thanks mostly to Blake's defense.

"Fatigue set in, but I can't blame it on that," Arrington said. "This is what you live for, to play the game of basketball. When you're out there, you have to forget about those things. Things went back their way. Momentum changed and never changed back."

And the Terps, despite a nearly invisible day from Chris Wilcox (four points, eight rebounds), rolled. Maryland converted 91 percent of its free throws and got 23 points from its bench, including eight points from freshman point guard Andre Collins in five minutes.

Next, the Terps will attempt to match the longest winning streak in school history by advancing to tomorrow's title game.

"We were really concerned with the way we were playing, but it happens to the best of us," Holden said. "We knew that, eventually, we'd make a run, too."

March 8, 2002: Florida State vs. MARYLAND

	1st	2nd	Total
Florida State	28	31	59
MARYLAND	40	45	85

Florida State

Player	FG-FGA	3-PT FG-FGA	FT-FTA	O-D REB	A	BLK	S	TP
04 Dixon, A	1-3	1-2	0-0	1-1	0	0	3	3
51 Waleskowski	0-2	0-0	0-0	2-3	0	0	2	0
34 Dixon, N	5-9	0-0	3-6	9-3	0	1	0	13
10 Arrington	3-13	1-6	2-4	0-2	4	0	2	9
30 Cummings	6-12	0-0	7-8	2-0	2	0	1	19
01 Joiner	0-6	0-2	0-0	0-2	1	0	0	0
03 Bracy	0-3	0-1	0-0	0-0	0	0	0	0
15 Harvey	1-5	0-0	5-5	3-0	0	1	0	7
21 Moran	0-0	0-0	0-0	0-0	0	0	0	0
23 Haywood	0-0	0-0	0-0	0-1	0	0	0	0
33 Mathews	0-0	0-0	0-0	0-0	0	0	0	0
44 Krieg	0-1	0-0	0-0	0-0	0	0	0	0
50 Anderson	0-0	0-0	0-0	0-0	0	0	0	0
54 Richardson	2-6	0-0	4-4	1-5	0	1	1	8

MARYLAND

Player	FG-FGA	3-PT FG-FGA	FT-FTA	O-D REB	A	BLK	S	TP
01 Mouton	5-9	0-1	8-8	6-1	2	0	0	18
54 Wilcox	1-7	0-0	2-2	2-6	0	0	0	4
35 Baxter	4-9	0-0	2-3	1-2	2	2	3	10
03 Dixon	7-14	3-6	3-4	2-3	4	1	2	20
25 Blake	4-6	2-4	0-0	1-4	7	0	5	10
05 McCall	1-1	0-0	0-0	1-1	0	0	0	2
10 Collins	3-3	0-0	2-2	0-1	1	0	1	8
12 Nicholas	1-4	0-3	1-1	0-1	2	0	0	3
21 Grinnon	0-0	0-0	0-0	0-0	0	0	0	0
33 Randle	2-4	0-0	2-2	1-1	0	3	0	6
45 Holden	2-5	0-1	0-0	1-0	1	0	0	4

NATIONAL CHAMPIONS

DOUG KAPUSTIN, THE BALTIMORE SUN

Off-Balance Three Pushes Teetering UM over the Edge

North Carolina State 86, Maryland 82

by CHRISTIAN EWELL

In the final 90 seconds of North Carolina State's 86-82 victory over Maryland, three players took NBA-range jump shots.

Two of the shots—from Drew Nicholas and Juan Dixon of Maryland—seemed to have plausible chances of going in. They missed. The third—from N.C. State's Julius Hodge—looked nothing like anything a shot doctor would prescribe. Of course, it went in.

"I don't mind a guy taking a nice-looking shot," a resigned Gary Williams said after his top-seeded team was upset in the Atlantic Coast Conference semifinals, "but that was unbelievable."

Such was Maryland's luck: being adequate but not quite good enough to answer this particular game's challenges from a team it had beaten twice, a team that was shooting 65 percent in the second half.

While the Terrapins were so unlike themselves—relying on Steve Blake's 21 points as their most reliable offensive firepower and getting so-so performances from the team's inside players—the Wolfpack displayed impeccable shooting for the second game in a row, hitting 11 three-pointers against the Terps after 13 against Virginia on Friday.

Off-balance, Hodge's jumper was taken about 23 feet away, Nicholas draped over him. The lead was at stake, a charging Maryland team cutting it from 13 to three.

Oh yeah, and the shot clock was about to run out, as his team's fans kept telling him.

"When I looked at the rim, I saw one second," he said. "Why not throw it up? This is March Madness. I had to make the shot."

So, with all the deliberation of someone who picks his winners for the NCAA tournament by school color, Hodge threw the ball up from the right wing, and the line drive went in, giving his team some much-needed breathing room and an 84-78 lead with 1:17 left to play.

"Great players do that," N.C. State coach Herb Sendek said. "Obviously that is not a part of our offense, but we'll take it."

NATIONAL CHAMPIONS

DOUG KAPUSTIN, THE BALTIMORE SUN

NATIONAL CHAMPIONS

When told of Hodge's claim that Nicholas' hand was on his shooting arm, Nicholas, a Long Island native, wrinkled his face skeptically before he said, "Us guys from New York know how to exaggerate," referring to Hodge's Bronx roots.

Baskets by Lonny Baxter and Blake and a bad pass by Anthony Grundy set the stage for long-range heroics from Maryland, which trailed 85-82 with 20 seconds left.

That's when Nicholas got his chance, taking the ball at a spot similar to where he got it twice during the Terrapins' comeback against Virginia on Jan. 31. Of course, he drained both from about six feet beyond the top of the key, and Maryland won.

This time, he missed the shot and the ball went out of bounds.

"I was pretty sure. It felt good coming out of my hand," Nicholas said. "Players have to take those kind of shots, and I'll take it again."

The same sentiment belonged to Dixon, whose attempt from the left wing also missed, going short and falling out of bounds despite Nicholas' effort to retrieve it.

That was Maryland's last gasp, with Grundy hitting a free throw in the last three seconds to seal the game.

"I thought it was a good look," Dixon said. "I probably could have gotten closer, but I missed. Next time, I'll hit it and take it from there."

"When I looked at the rim, I saw one second. Why not throw it up? This is March Madness. I had to make the shot."
N.C. STATE'S JULIUS HODGE

NATIONAL CHAMPIONS

DOUG KAPUSTIN, THE BALTIMORE SUN

117

March 9, 2002 : NC State vs. MARYLAND

	1st	2nd	Total
NC State	40	46	86
MARYLAND	38	44	82

NC State

Player	FG-FGA	3-PT FG-FGA	FT-FTA	O-D REB	A	BLK	S	TP
24 Hodge	6-8	1-2	1-3	0-1	5	0	3	14
33 Powell	0-1	0-0	0-0	1-1	0	0	0	0
54 Melvin	7-12	4-8	1-4	1-5	3	0	0	19
02 Grundy	9-12	2-4	4-7	1-7	4	0	1	24
11 Miller	3-7	3-7	7-8	1-3	3	0	2	16
03 Evtimov	4-7	1-4	3-4	0-2	5	0	1	12
23 Sherrill	0-2	0-2	0-0	0-1	0	0	0	0
30 Crawford	0-0	0-0	1-2	0-2	2	0	0	1
32 Collins	0-0	0-0	0-0	1-0	0	0	0	0

MARYLAND

Player	FG-FGA	3-PT FG-FGA	FT-FTA	O-D REB	A	BLK	S	TP
01 Mouton	1-5	0-1	7-8	3-4	3	0	2	9
54 Wilcox	6-14	0-0	3-4	1-2	2	1	1	15
35 Baxter	6-9	0-0	3-3	3-4	0	0	1	15
03 Dixon	6-16	1-4	0-0	1-2	2	0	0	13
25 Blake	7-9	2-4	5-6	0-5	11	0	6	21
12 Nicholas	2-5	1-4	2-2	1-1	1	0	0	7
33 Randle	0-1	0-0	0-0	0-1	0	1	0	0
45 Holden	1-2	0-1	0-0	1-1	1	0	1	2

NATIONAL CHAMPIONS

COLE: THANKS FOR THE MEMORIES 1955-2002

TERPS NEW CHAMPS AROUND ACC

IXON YOUR MOUTH

Terps Take First Step, Sink Siena
Dixon's 29 Points Lift Top Seed by No. 16, 85-70

by GARY LAMBRECHT

The Maryland Terrapins did not exactly walk all over 16th-seeded Siena from start to finish, but the Terps still moved on to their next NCAA tournament test with relative ease.

Led by senior guard Juan Dixon, who moved within seven points of the all-time school scoring record held by Len Bias with a game-high and season-high 29 points, top-seeded Maryland began its trip through the East Regional by whipping Siena, 85-70, before 18,770 at MCI Center. The Terps, who had a 13-game winning streak broken by North Carolina State in last week's Atlantic Coast Conference tournament semifinals, started what they hoped will be a six-game winning streak that culminates with the school's first national championship.

Maryland (27-4), which enjoyed a decided home-crowd advantage some 20 minutes from its campus, will face eighth-seeded Wisconsin in the NCAA's second round. With a victory, the Terps would advance to their sixth Sweet 16 round in the last nine seasons.

Maryland was the last No. 1 seed to play in the tournament and a No. 1 seed has never lost in the first round, which wasn't lost on Gary Williams and his players.

"This was a little different for us, sitting around for two days and watching everybody else play," Williams said. "I think there was pressure on the players, whether they admit it or not. We've been hearing for two days how a No. 1 seed has never lost in the first round. How do you explain it if you lose this game? What do you say? I'm going to Mexico? You can't go to Disneyland."

Maryland began its ninth straight trip to the NCAAs by facing a team with the only losing record in the tournament, and Siena (17-19) actually put up an admirable fight for a while. But it was only a matter of time before Maryland began to outclass the Saints with its size, speed, strength and pedigree.

"We really threw a pretty good punch at [Siena] early in the game, the way we ran our offense. And they came right back and matched us," Williams said. "That was pretty impressive. They made us work, which was good. We won, that's what's important. We got [the lead] to 20 and couldn't sustain it. We played very good defense [at times], but we didn't sustain it. Siena has some good shooters. You have to keep trying to get better, even in the NCAA tournament."

NATIONAL CHAMPIONS

UM Gets Serious, 87-57

Terps Slice Wisconsin as Dixon Hits 29 Again to Stroll Into Sweet 16

by GARY LAMBRECHT

The Maryland Terrapins had too much at stake and too many weapons for this contest to play out any other way.

Start with senior guard Juan Dixon, who gave the home crowd everything it wanted at MCI Center by scoring a game-high 29 points and setting a school career scoring record. Move on to sophomore forward Chris Wilcox, whose power moves and dunks energized the fans and his teammates. Throw in the Terps' withering defensive pressure, inside brawn and the desire to play the game at their speed. Wisconsin might have thought and hoped it had a chance for a while, but five minutes into the second half of Maryland's 87-57 East Regional rout of the eighth-seeded Badgers, the top-seeded Terps already had removed all doubt about which team was moving on from the NCAA tournament's second round.

The Terps, looking more businesslike and determined than they have in more than a week, brought their Final Four faces to the court, not to mention a superior collection of experienced talent.

And after taking control of the game in the closing minutes of the first half, then knocking out the Badgers with a 17-3 run to open the second half, Maryland is two victories away from making its second consecutive trip to college basketball's biggest stage.

Maryland (28-4), which is going to the Sweet 16 for the sixth time in the past nine years under coach Gary Williams, will face fourth-seeded Kentucky on Friday night in the East Regional semifinals at the Carrier Dome in Syracuse, N.Y. The Terps tuned up for their trip north by recording the most lopsided victory in the school's NCAA tournament history.

"I think we feel like we are unbeatable right now," said Dixon, who needed seven points to pass the late Len Bias as Maryland's all-time leading scorer and matched his 29-point effort in Maryland's opening-round victory over Siena. "With confidence like that, we can go a long way and right now we feel like we are unstoppable."

"The thing about our team, from Juan Dixon on, is that everybody is about winning," Williams said. "We are going to win the game any way we can, and that was our attitude

---

NATIONAL CHAMPIONS

NATIONAL CHAMPIONS

Terps Shoot by Kentucky Into Great 8

Free Throws, Defense Move Top Seed Past Kentucky, 78-68

by GARY LAMBRECHT

The Maryland Terrapins were not as sharp as they wanted to be, but they were plenty good enough to push their way into the coveted Elite Eight round of the NCAA tournament for the second straight year.

Top seed Maryland overcame bouts with turnovers, some shaky shot selection and a subpar showing by point guard Steve Blake, not to mention a physical, determined Kentucky opponent that wore down in the closing minutes. But the Terps played excellent defense, made their free throws in the clutch, wore down Kentucky inside in the second half and did enough dirty work to move one victory from their second consecutive trip to the Final Four by pulling away to a 78-68 victory in the East Regional semifinals before 29,633 at the Carrier Dome.

The Terps (29-4), who achieved a single-season school record for victories, will face second-seeded Connecticut in the regional final, with the winner advancing to next week's national semifinals in Atlanta.

Maryland beat the Huskies, 77-65, to win the BB&T Classic in early December.

"It was a great effort. We just didn't execute. We made some bad plays, but we knew what we were doing," Maryland coach Gary Williams said. "You know what's good about this team? It didn't take away from our defensive effort. It was a defensive game. As long as we kept playing good defense, we knew we had a chance to win the game. We turned the ball over, the shots weren't falling, but we got the ball inside in the second half."

Maryland clinched the victory over the fourth-seeded Wildcats (22-10) by making 21 of 24 free throws, including 14 of 15 attempts in the second half. The Terps eliminated the Wildcats by putting together a game-closing 12-5 run, after Kentucky had closed to 66-63 with 5:05 left.

Maryland also did it with scoring balance. Senior guard Juan Dixon, who got the Terps rolling early, led the way with 19 points. Senior center Lonny Baxter had 16 points,

---

NATIONAL CHAMPIONS

including 14 in the second half. Sophomore power forward Chris Wilcox had 15 points, and senior forward Byron Mouton complemented a superb defensive job on Kentucky forward Tayshaun Prince by scoring 14 points.

"Kentucky is a great team. They play in one of the best conferences in the country, and they came out with a lot of fight tonight. But I think we wanted it just a little more," Dixon said. "We had some scoring balance. Our big guys won the game for us in the second half. And we played.

KENNETH K. LAM, THE BALTIMORE SUN

Blake Answers Call for Ball with a Shot from Long Distance

Guard's 3, His Lone Basket, Cuts Off UConn's Hopes

by PAUL MCMULLEN

Two huge East Regional games, two nights in which Maryland players who were suffering through subpar games asked for the ball.

On Friday, it was Lonny Baxter going against character and demanding the ball at halftime against Kentucky. Held to two points in the first half, Baxter got 14 in the second. Against Connecticut, it was Steve Blake who piped up, asking for the ball and producing an improbable three-pointer that sealed the Terps' 90-82 victory in the regional final of the NCAA basketball tournament. With 25.4 seconds left and the shot clock about to expire, Blake nailed a three that extended the Terps' lead to 86-80. It was his only field goal of the game. Plagued by early foul trouble, Blake didn't attempt a shot in the first 33 minutes, but he pleaded for the ball during a tense timeout with 34 seconds remaining.

Juan Dixon and Baxter are go-to guys, but Connecticut was clamping down on the center in the second half and the Huskies were sure to pay close attention to the All-America guard, whom three minutes earlier had triggered a classic display of clutch offense with a three-pointer of his own. Blake interrupted coach

Gary Williams as he diagrammed a play for Dixon.

"At the timeout, we were trying to get Juan a look," Williams said, "but Steve said, `They're going to play those guys and I think I can get a shot.' I said, `Go ahead and take it.' I didn't think he was going to take it from that far out, but Blake's done that a lot for us, making big shots."

Blake, who did not commit a turnover and had six assists to build his school career record to 737, acknowledged the weight of the moment. "That was probably my biggest shot to seal a game," the junior point guard said. "It came at a point where it put a dagger in them. I like to take those kinds of shots."

In addition to the late threes by Blake and Dixon, one other Maryland three-pointer deflated Connecticut. With two seconds left in the first half, junior forward Tahj Holden hit a jumper from the top of the key that gave the Terps a 44-37 lead. The shot evoked last year's West Regional final, when Holden's three in front of the Stanford bench gave Maryland a 10-point lead at the break.

NATIONAL CHAMPIONS

The three was only Holden's second in the Terps' past eight games. He finished with eight points, his most since January. Holden's second best point total of the season came against.

Clutch Terps

Pushed to Brink, UM Rides Baxter, Dixon by UConn to Final 4

by GARY LAMBRECHT

Senior forward Byron Mouton seemed to be laughing and crying at the same time. Senior center Lonny Baxter looked exhausted, as a man should after carrying a team for extended periods of time. Senior guard Juan Dixon had just produced 39 incredible minutes filled with energy, heart and desire, and he sounded ready to take and make one more shot with the season hanging in the balance.

At so many points in the contest, the Maryland Terrapins appeared ripe for a fall in the NCAA tournament's East Regional championship game. The Terps ran into foul trouble at several positions, took a seven-point halftime lead that would not last long, and seemed to be helpless in the face of the powerful play of Connecticut sophomore Caron Butler and the slashing athleticism of those Huskies guards.

But the Terps did what the great basketball teams do. They refused to waver, refused to stop believing they would play for one more weekend, refused to accept a premature end to the course they have plotted for a year. And veterans like Dixon and Baxter saw to it that Maryland would not be silenced.

In what had to be the most pulsating contest produced in this NCAA tournament so far, top-seeded Maryland rode the hulking shoulders of Baxter and the killer instinct of Dixon to its second consecutive Final Four appearance by overtaking a dogged Connecticut team in the final two minutes and closing out a 90-82 victory before 29,252 who got their money's worth and then some at the Carrier Dome.

The victory completes phase one of a yearlong mission. Maryland (30-4), which already has achieved the best record in school history and has won 30 games in a season for the first time, advanced as the No. 1 seed to the national semifinal round at the Georgia Dome in Atlanta, where on Saturday night the Terps will face Kansas, the Midwest Regional winner and also a top seed.

The winner will play either Oklahoma or Indiana on Monday night for the national championship.

"Just getting there is hard either way," junior point guard Steve Blake said of a return trip to the game's ultimate stage. "It's been a great year so far. We're not satisfied with getting there. We want to win the whole thing."

NATIONAL CHAMPIONS

"This is too much fun. Nobody back home wanted me to come to the University of Maryland," said a beaming Mouton, who hails from Rayne, La., and elected to transfer from Tulane after two seasons, then sat out for a year in College Park before hitting the court as a Terp last season.

"Everybody wanted me to go to Kentucky or UConn because of all of their tradition. I went to the Final Four last year, won an ACC championship and am going back to the Final Four this year. Two-for-two, not bad at all. I'm a part of history."

Dixon and Baxter certainly created some history. Baxter, the shy, soft-spoken, 6-foot-8 senior who has been the foundation of Maryland's offense for three seasons, earned a regional Most Outstanding Player award for the second straight year by shredding the Huskies inside with a season-high 29 points and a game-high nine rebounds.

Dixon, the slender 6-3 guard from East Baltimore who has defied personal tragedy and the low expectations that greeted him when he arrived at Maryland nearly five years ago and already is the leading scorer in school history, left them roaring last night with 27 points and clutch moments that have long been his signature.

It was an epic struggle that produced 24 lead changes and 21 ties. It was also a night when the younger Huskies, coached by the wily Jim Calhoun—who engaged in an intriguing chess match with Williams of switching defenses and protecting foul-plagued players—pushed Maryland to the brink of defeat while riding the talent of Butler.

He scored 26 of his game-high 32 points in the second half, grabbed a team-high seven rebounds and looked like an underclassman about to leave early for the NBA.

But Dixon, with help from Baxter and a huge lift from Blake, who had struggled mightily in the regional semifinal victory over Kentucky, made sure the Terps came out smiling. With Connecticut protecting a 77-74 lead, Dixon demanded the ball and demanded the chance to make victory happen.

And he delivered once again, by burying a three-point shot from the top of the key in the face of Huskies guard Taliek Brown to tie the score at 77 with 3:43 remaining. That fueled a sequence during which Maryland scored on its final eight possessions and showed its composure by hitting its last eight foul shots.

Dixon would make four free throws down the stretch. Baxter would score four points. And Blake would ice the game with a three-pointer with 25.4 seconds left. His lone field goal of the game put the Terps on top 86-80.

"I didn't want this to be my last game. I never showed that much emotion in my life," said Dixon, who pumped his fist and swung his arm in windmill-like fashion after sinking the earlier tying three. "This is the last time I get to go through this. There was no way this was going to be our last game."

"There had to be a way to win that game, and we found it," Williams said. "It's a credit to these guys, because it didn't look good, especially when UConn took the lead there. We never faltered on what we were trying to do. To watch [Dixon and Baxter] play, especially now, I don't think there's ever been a better class at the university."

#	PF	PTS	MARYLAND
01	2	4	
03	3	20	**74**
12	1	2	
35	2	25	TOL 2
54	4	13	10 TEAM FOUL

3:4

PERIOD 2
POSSESSI

Carrier CARRIER DOME

GIONA
TY

MAR
SOUT

One To Go

Terps Hold Off Big Rally by Kansas, Will Meet Indiana for NCAA title

by GARY LAMBRECHT

I t's no longer a dream, no longer a goal they have been obsessed with reaching for past year.

The Maryland Terrapins are about to play for the first national championship in school history. Last night before 53,378 at the Georgia Dome, the Terps overcame a night when senior star center Lonny Baxter was nearly invisible with foul trouble, battled through a game in which they nearly blew a 20-point second-half lead, and never stopped pushing until they eliminated the Kansas Jayhawks in the NCAA tournament semifinals, 97-88.

Maryland, after riding a career-high 33 points from guard Juan Dixon and outstanding efforts from forwards Chris Wilcox and Tahj Holden, will make its first appearance in the NCAA championship game when it faces Indiana tomorrow night.

What a night it was for the Terps (31-4) to show the talent, depth and heart that has made this the best team in school history. What a night it was for the Terps, who stared down the team many had picked to win the tournament, even after Maryland stumbled late by watching an 83-63 lead shrink to 92-88 with 20 seconds left.

And what a night it was for Dixon, who managed to top his first two superb weekends of NCAA tournament play with his best effort yet.

Dixon, the leading scorer in school history, continued his torrid March shooting by making 10 of 18 shots, including five of 11 from three-point range. He scored 19 points in the first half, when Maryland stormed back to turn a 13-2 deficit into a 44-37 halftime lead.

Dixon added 14 in the second half, including six points in the final 1:11 to help the Terps avoid a collapse that no doubt made Maryland fans recall last year's Final Four flop against Duke. The Terps blew a 22-point first-half lead in the semifinals before losing to the eventual national champions.

This time, Maryland closed the deal for its 18th victory in the past 19 games by handing Kansas (33-4) only its second defeat since Jan. 12.

NATIONAL CHAMPIONS

Big Men Wilcox, Holden Rise to Challenge Up Front

Two Terps Combine to Score 31, Neutralize Kansas' Inside Game

by CHRISTIAN EWELL

Faced with perhaps its toughest frontcourt challenge of the season, Maryland dominated down low during a 97-88 victory over Kansas and did so in an unexpected fashion.

Kansas All-America center Drew Gooden was a non-factor for much of the game, not recording a second-half field goal until 7:22 remained in the game. But Maryland's dynamite performance didn't come from Lonny Baxter—who was the Most Outstanding Performer of the East Regional. Baxter was hampered by foul trouble for much of the game and finished with just four points.

Instead, it was Chris Wilcox and Tahj Holden who combined for 31 points to go along with Juan Dixon's 33 points and move the Terrapins into the national title game against Indiana.

The pair wanted to avenge what they saw as an affront to their talents from Gooden, who had said that he and Nick Collison were the best frontcourt duo in the nation.

"He's a great player, but I had to take it personally," Wilcox said, "because he said that they were the best in the land. I wanted to let them know that there are at least two others in that race."

This isn't the first time Wilcox has come through against big-name competition. In February, he had 23 points and 11 rebounds against Carlos Boozer in Maryland's convincing 87-73 victory over Duke.

At stake was not only Maryland's quest for a national championship, but also a test for Wilcox's readiness for the NBA. Gooden, like Wilcox, is considered a likely lottery pick for the league's draft this summer.

Wilcox did nothing to calm that suggestion, with 11 points and six rebounds in the first half, en route to an 18-point, nine-rebound night that also included four blocks.

He also had three blocked shots in the first five minutes of the game—all on attempts by Gooden—to set a tone that reverberated from

---

NATIONAL CHAMPIONS

then on. Collison was the only Jayhawk to go inside with any confidence.

"Wilcox kind of set the tone early by blocking so many shots," Collison said. "Tahj Holden came in, played a great game. I give them a lot of credit."

Holden, who finished with 13 points and five rebounds, is used to putting out fires whenever Baxter or Wilcox get into foul trouble. But instead of serving as a mere stopgap, the junior from New Jersey stepped forward, with six of those points in the first half, eliminating the question of what would happen without Baxter.

Later, Holden's tip-in with 8:55 left in the game gave the Terps a 73-59 lead and began an 11-4 run that was all the cushion they would need.

"You don't know how the others are going to step up," teammate Byron Mouton said. "But when Tahj got his first basket . . . all we wanted was for him to be aggressive. I've never seen him flying through the air like that."

"At this point, I've seen everything—it's happened before, and I had to go in and play," said Holden, who admitted to a little fatigue because of the up-and-down style of play.

"I gave everything for as long as I could. I was just determined not to let them beat me up the court, not to let them score. Sometimes, those things [fatigue] go away when you're determined."

> **I gave everything for as long as I could. I was just determined not to let them beat me up the court, not to let them score. Sometimes, those things [fatigue] go away when you're determined.**
>
> TERPS JUNIOR FORWARD TAHJ HOLDEN

LLOYD FOX, THE BALTIMORE SUN

March 30, 2002: Kansas vs. MARYLAND

	1st	2nd	Total
Kansas	37	51	88
MARYLAND	44	53	97

Kansas

Player	FG-FGA	3-PT FG-FGA	FT-FTA	O-D REB	A	BLK	S	TP
04 Collison	9-14	0-0	3-4	3-7	1	1	1	21
00 Gooden	5-12	2-2	3-5	3-6	3	1	1	15
10 Hinrich	4-8	2-3	1-2	0-4	4	0	1	11
11 Miles	1-7	0-4	10-12	1-2	10	0	2	12
13 Boschee	6-16	5-13	0-0	0-3	2	0	1	17
03 Ballard	0-0	0-0	0-0	0-0	0	0	0	0
05 Langford	2-6	0-1	4-8	1-4	2	0	0	8
22 Carey	0-1	0-0	0-0	0-0	0	0	0	0
23 Simien	2-3	0-0	0-0	2-3	0	1	0	4

MARYLAND

Player	FG-FGA	3-PT FG-FGA	FT-FTA	O-D REB	A	BLK	S	TP
01 Mouton	4-9	0-0	4-4	3-3	2	0	1	12
54 Wilcox	8-15	0-0	2-3	3-6	1	4	1	18
35 Baxter	2-4	0-0	0-0	2-5	0	2	1	4
03 Dixon	10-18	5-11	8-11	0-3	2	0	2	33
25 Blake	1-7	1-4	5-9	0-3	11	0	1	8
12 Nicholas	2-9	1-5	2-2	0-2	2	0	0	7
33 Randle	1-3	0-0	0-1	1-1	0	2	0	2
45 Holden	4-5	0-1	5-5	2-3	0	1	1	13

NATIONAL CHAMPIONS

KARL MERTON FERRON, THE BALTIMORE SUN

UM Grinds Out Victory, Earns National Title

Maryland Pulls Away Late to Top Dogged Hoosiers, Win First National Crown

by GARY LAMBRECHT

The final buzzer sounded, Juan Dixon and Lonny Baxter tumbled to the Georgia Dome floor locked in a joyous embrace, and the Maryland Terrapins had completed their historic journey by winning the first men's national basketball championship in school history.

The Terps have shown their mettle in so many ways throughout this marvelous season, and the Indiana Hoosiers brought out yet another layer of toughness in Maryland. Indiana used tenacious defense and outside shooting to push the Terps to the brink of a stunning upset.

But in the end, the Terps were too strong for the upstart Hoosiers, who brought a Cinderella story to Atlanta in search of their sixth NCAA crown. In the end, the senior tandem of Dixon and Baxter and Maryland's size and stubborn will carried the evening, as the Terps pulled away in the final eight minutes of a ragged affair to beat Indiana, 64-52, before 53,406.

The victory turned the court into a party scene, which culminated with the Terps cutting down the nets for the third and final time this season. Dixon, who was named the Final Four's Most Outstanding Player by a unanimous vote after leading the Terps with 18 points and finishing the NCAA tournament with 155, cut the final strand of one net and flung it about 30 feet to a group of his teammates.

Coach Gary Williams, who finally got to taste the game's sweetest fruit after laboring for 24 seasons, including the past 13 at Maryland, twirled the other net several times and pumped his fist at the Terps faithful in the stands behind the team bench. Minutes later, Williams, wearing a NCAA championship cap, held his grandson at midcourt.

"This is a great thrill. We really had to grind," Williams said. "We had to go through some great teams to get here, and Indiana played some great defense on us. The players hung in there. I'm really proud of them. I've never done this before, so I'm not sure what I'm supposed to be like. I'm really happy. But I'm really tired."

NATIONAL CHAMPIONS

Fittingly, Maryland (32-4), which closed the season by winning 19 of its last 20 games, had to dig down deep to get it done. The Terps started fast, bolting to a 23-11 lead, as they ruled the inside with the bulk of Baxter and Chris Wilcox and the outside touch of Dixon. But Indiana, which had relied on three-point shooting and defense while winning the South Regional as a No. 5 seed, refused to fade without a fight.

Indiana (25-12) trailed for nearly all of the game's first 30 minutes before inching ahead 44-42 on a layup by forward Jared Jeffries with 9:53 left. But that's when Dixon and Baxter stepped up to pull the Terps over the hump and into the history books.

Dixon, who was held in check by guard Dane Fife without a point for nearly a 20-minute stretch spanning both halves, did what he has done for three years. He hit the big shots. First, he broke his scoring drought by taking a feed from point guard Steve Blake and making a 23-foot three-point shot from the left wing to put the Terps back in front 45-44.

Then, after Baxter made two free throws to pad the lead, Dixon answered a 15-foot jumper by Fife with a spectacular 18-foot fall-away to put Maryland on top 49-46 with 8:11 left. With that, Maryland was off on a 17-3 run that would seal a hard-earned crown.

"I am so proud of everyone on this team. Lonny and me beat the odds and led our team to a title," Dixon said. "I can't put into words how excited I am now. I'm speechless."

"We definitely wanted to give Coach a ring," said Baxter, who atoned for his ineffective, foul-marred semifinal performance against Kansas on Saturday night by recording 15 points and game highs of 14 rebounds and three blocked shots. "He came in and turned around the program tremendously. It's about time he got what he deserved."

This was far from a classic victory. But Maryland did the dirty work to finish the season in the only way it could have envisioned. The Terps wore down the Hoosiers on the boards with their muscle, grabbing 46 rebounds to Indiana's 32. Maryland made 20 of 28 free throws, including nine of its last 10.

The Terps won with senior forward Byron Mouton keeping key loose balls alive in the closing minutes with tremendous hustle. They won with five different players putting away the game on the foul line. They won by maintaining their composure in the face of another dogged opponent.

"I'm tired, but I'm more relieved than tired. It's a big relief, winning this championship we wanted since last year," said junior forward Tahj Holden. "It would have crushed me probably if we didn't win."

"I'm at the point where you're so happy you could cry. I hope everybody in this room at some point can feel like this," said Drew Nicholas, Maryland's junior backup guard. "This is about growing up, going to college and becoming a man. It doesn't get any better than this.

The Hoosiers, who were outplayed decisively during the game's first 10 minutes, fed off a 14-8 run that closed the first half, fed off of their three-point shooters, and capitalized on a turnover-prone Maryland offense to forge a 40-40 tie with 11:43 left in the contest. That was the first tie since 2-2.

Jeffries then schooled Wilcox on back-to-back possessions by beating him for layups, the

second of which gave the Hoosiers their first lead of the game at 44-42 with 9:53 left.

It didn't last, because Dixon reawakened by hitting the biggest shot of the game. His three-pointer from the left wing put the Terps back in front 45-44 with 9:41 to go.

"I was trying to be patient," Dixon said of his key basket. "Let the game come to me. Steve [Blake] set me up and I made a big shot."

Not that Indiana went quietly. After Baxter made two free throws, Fife's 15-footer pulled the Hoosiers to 47-46, but the Terps responded with a 17-3 run that gave them a 64-49 lead with 1:43 left. Fueling the decisive run was a 9-for-10 show at the free-throw line by five different players.

ELIZABETH MALBY, THE BALTIMORE SUN

NATIONAL CHAMPIONS

Take Bow, Champs, for All Terps Who Didn't

by MIKE PRESTON

The University of Maryland put its name in the history books and brought a championship banner to College Park as the Terps officially became an elite member of college basketball.

It wasn't pretty. Actually, it may have been one of the ugliest championship games in NCAA history as Maryland defeated Indiana, 64-52, before a crowd of 53,406 at the Georgia Dome to capture its first national title.

But who cares about cosmetics?

The Terps did what they had to do. They did what Len Bias, Keith Booth and Steve Francis couldn't do. They succeeded where Tom McMillen and Len Elmore failed. Buck and Albert didn't get it done, and Lefty never lived up to his promise of making Maryland the UCLA of the East.

Oh, what a run.

To win its first national championship, Maryland ran through some of the most storied programs in college basketball. The Terps beat Kentucky and Connecticut in the regionals, and Kansas and Indiana in the Final Four. That's three of the best coaches in the game, too, in Tubby Smith, Jim Calhoun and Roy Williams.

It's no wonder Terps players hugged at the final horn with forward Chris Wilcox hugging point guard Steve Blake, and then hoisting him high in the air.

Heroes?

The entire team.

Most Valuable Player? Juan Dixon, who else?

"I don't think that anyone can guard him one-on-one," Indiana forward Kyle Hornsby said.

The senior shooting guard from Baltimore and Calvert Hall high school finished with 18 points, hitting six of nine from the field and four of four from the foul line. In the tournament, Dixon scored 29, 29, 19, 27, 33 and 18 points. No one in the past five years

NATIONAL CHAMPIONS

has carried a team through a tournament like Dixon.

There were times here at the Final Four that he became an assistant coach, but he never overstepped his bounds. The final curtain call belonged to head coach Gary Williams, whose program was on life support when he first took over 13 years ago.

"This is a great thrill," Williams said. "Not many coaches get a chance to coach three great seniors [Dixon, Byron Mouton and Lonny Baxter] like this. It was a thrill for me to watch these guys work this hard and get their reward. There were a lot of people involved in this. It took all our administration, our staff and everyone involved with the program to make this happen."

Minutes before the Terps were presented with the national championship plaque, Maryland fans chanted Williams' name, and then followed it with a chorus of "We're No. 1."

This was a team built in the mold of Williams. Intense, confident and with a chip on its shoulders. After blowing a 22-point lead to Duke last year in the Final Four semifinals, every one of them said they had only one goal, and that was to win a national championship.

And they never blinked under pressure.

There were some nervous moments last night. Blake was erratic again as he has been in the postseason. Wilcox and Baxter looked tired in the first half, and reserve forward Tahj Holden got into foul trouble.

But with the score 51-46, Holden made two foul shots with 5:04 remaining. Reserve guard Drew Nicholas made it 55-49 on a layup with 3:33 left. Baxter converted one of two foul shots 30 seconds later, and Dixon made two more foul shots with 2:43 remaining.

When Blake converted two foul shots with 2:13 left to put Maryland ahead 60-49, it was goodbye Hoosiers, hello national championship.

Baxter finished with 15 points and 14 rebounds, 12 on the defensive end. Wilcox added 10 points and seven rebounds. Typical Maryland. The Terps have been balanced all year, a team with no superstars, just role players and underachievers who turned the Terps into the nation's best college basketball team in 2002.

"I am so proud of everyone on this team," Dixon said. "Lonny and me beat the odds and led our team to a title. I can't put into words how excited I am now. Coach Williams took a chance on me and I thank him for that. This has been a great experience."

"This is the greatest feeling," Holden said. "This is exactly what we've worked hard all year for. It wasn't pretty, but we had guys making plays when we had to."

"This is a great thrill. Not many coaches get a chance to coach three great seniors [Dixon, Byron Mouton and Lonny Baxter] like this. It was a thrill for me to watch these guys work this hard and get their reward."

TERPS HEAD COACH GARY WILLIAMS

KENNETH K. LAM, THE BALTIMORE SUN

153

April 1, 2002: Indiana vs. MARYLAND

	1st	2nd	Total
Indiana	25	27	52
MARYLAND	31	33	64

Indiana

Player	FG-FGA	3-PT FG-FGA	FT-FTA	O-D REB	A	BLK	S	TP
01 Jeffries	4-11	0-1	0-1	1-6	3	1	1	8
32 Hornsby	5-12	4-8	0-1	2-3	0	0	2	14
43 Odle	0-4	0-0	0-3	1-3	1	0	1	0
03 Coverdale	3-11	2-7	0-0	0-4	2	0	2	8
11 Fife	4-9	3-6	0-0	2-3	1	0	2	11
02 Moye	1-1	0-0	0-0	0-0	0	0	1	2
05 Leach	0-0	0-0	0-0	0-0	0	1	0	0
12 Perry	1-3	1-1	0-0	0-1	0	0	0	3
50 Newton	2-7	0-0	2-2	3-2	2	1	1	6

MARYLAND

Player	FG-FGA	3-PT FG-FGA	FT-FTA	O-D REB	A	BLK	S	TP
01 Mouton	1-5	0-0	2-2	2-2	1	1	2	4
54 Wilcox	4-8	0-0	2-4	2-5	0	1	1	10
35 Baxter	6-15	0-0	3-8	2-12	0	3	1	15
03 Dixon	6-9	2-4	4-4	1-4	3	0	5	18
25 Blake	2-6	0-3	2-2	0-6	3	0	2	6
12 Nicholas	1-2	0-1	5-6	1-2	0	0	1	7
33 Randle	1-1	0-0	0-0	0-0	0	0	0	2
45 Holden	0-2	0-1	2-2	1-2	4	1	0	2

KARL MERTON FERRON, THE BALTIMORE SUN

2001-02 SEASON STATISTICS

PLAYER	GP	FG-FGA	3-PT FG-FGA	FT-FTA	O REB	D REB	A	BLK	STL	TP	AVG
03 Dixon, J	36	251-535	92-232	141-157	49	117	104	7	92	735	20.4
35 Baxter, L	35	193-354	0-1	147-236	80	208	28	69	33	533	15.2
54 Wilcox, C	36	173-343	0-2	86-147	97	160	53	53	28	432	12.0
01 Mouton, B	36	144-307	14-55	99-129	89	91	74	6	34	401	11.1
25 Blake, S	36	91-238	44-128	61-74	20	117	286	16	56	287	8.0
12 Nicholas, D	36	82-172	38-96	53-66	10	71	88	12	16	255	7.1
45 Holden, T	36	62-137	17-40	61-73	32	64	42	34	21	202	5.6
33 Randle, R	34	55-105	1-1	18-32	35	71	5	18	13	129	3.8
10 Collins, A	22	18-27	5-10	7-9	0	12	19	0	5	48	2.2
05 McCall, C	19	10-19	5-10	2-4	1	14	2	1	3	27	1.4
21 Grinnon, M	16	2-7	1-4	2-2	3	2	4	0	1	7	0.4
04 Badu, E	12	2-4	0-1	0-4	0	3	9	0	0	4	0.3

NATIONAL CHAMPIONS

SEASON RESULTS

Date	Opponent	Site	Result
Nov. 2	EA Sports All-Stars (Exh.)	College Park, MD	W 98-80
Nov. 8	Arizona (IKON Classic)	New York, NY	L 67-71
Nov. 9	Temple (IKON Classic)	New York, NY	W 82-74
Nov. 13	NIKE Elite (exh.)	College Park, MD	W 99-67
Nov. 17	American	College Park, MD	W 83-53
Nov. 24	Deleware State	College Park, MD	W 77-53
Nov. 27	Illinois (ACC/Big Ten Challenge)	College Park, MD	W 76-63
Dec. 2	Princeton (BB&T Classic)	Washington, DC	W 61-53
Dec. 3	Connecticut (BB&T Classic)	Washington, DC	W 77-65
Dec. 9	Detroit	College Park, MD	W 79-54
Dec. 11	Monmouth	College Park, MD	W 91-55
Dec. 21	Oklahoma	Norman, OK	L 56-72
Dec. 27	William & Mary	College Park, MD	W 103-75
Dec. 30	NC State	Raleigh, NC	W 72-65
Jan. 3	Norfolk State	College Park, MD	W 92-69
Jan. 9	North Carolina	College Park, MD	W 112-79
Jan. 13	Georgia Tech	Atlanta, GA	W 92-87
Jan. 17	Duke	Durham, NC	L 78-99
Jan. 20	Clemson	College Park, MD	W 99-90
Jan. 23	Wake Forest	Winston-Salem, NC	W 85-63
Jan. 26	Florida State	College Park, MD	W 84-63
Jan. 31	Virginia	Charlottesville, VA	W 91-87
Feb. 3	NC State	College Park, MD	W 89-73
Feb. 10	North Carolina	Chapel Hill, NC	W 92-77
Feb. 13	Georgia Tech	College Park, MD	W 85-65
Feb. 17	Duke	College Park, MD	W 87-73
Feb. 20	Clemson	Clemson, SC	W 84-68
Feb. 24	Wake Forest	College Park, MD	W 90-89
Feb. 27	Florida State	Tallahassee, FL	W 96-63
Mar. 3	Virginia	College Park, MD	W 112-92
Mar. 8	Florida State (ACC Tourn.)	Charlotte, NC	W 85-59
Mar. 9	NC State (ACC Tourn.)	Charlotte, NC	L 82-86
Mar. 15	Siena College (NCAA Tourn.)	Washington, DC	W 85-70
Mar. 17	Wisconsin (NCAA Tourn.)	Washington, DC	W 87-57
Mar. 22	Kentucky (NCAA Tourn.)	Syracuse, NY	W 78-68
Mar. 24	Connecticut (NCAA Tourn.)	Syracuse, NY	W 90-82
Mar. 30	Kansas (NCAA Tourn.)	Atlanta, GA	W 97-88
Apr. 1	Indiana (NCAA Tourn.)	Atlanta, GA	W 64-52

DOUG KAPUSTIN, THE BALTIMORE SUN

ACKNOWLEDGMENTS

The entire staff of the BALTIMORE SUN contributed to the coverage
of the 2001-2002 University of Maryland men's basketball national championship season. We gratefully
acknowledge the efforts of the Photography and Sports Departments.

PHOTOGRAPHY DEPARTMENT

PHOTOGRAPHERS: Andre Chung, Amy Davis, Karl Merton Ferron, Lloyd Fox,
Barbara Haddock-Taylor, Kim Hairston, Nanine Hartzenbusch, David Hobby,
Doug Kapustin, Chiaki Kawajiri, Jed Kirschbaum, Ken Lam,
Monica Lopossay-Reisser, John Makely, Elizabeth Malby, Algerina Perna and Gene Sweeney, Jr.

PHOTO TECHICIANS: Danielle Bradley, Julie Ferguson and Denise Sanders

PHOTO EDITORS: Glenn Fawcett, Jerry Jackson, Rissa Miller,
Weyman Swagger, Chuck Weiss and Linda White

CHIEF PHOTO EDITOR: Eileen Ryan
ASSISTANT DIR. OF PHOTOGRAPHY: Jeff Bill
DEPUTY DIR. OF PHOTOGRAPHY: David Lewis
DIR. OF PHOTOGRAPHY: Robert K. Hamilton
ASSISTANT MANAGING EDITOR OF PHOTOGRAPHY: Jim Preston

SPORTS DEPARTMENT

EDITORS: Sam Davis, Patricia Fanning, Ray Frager, Steve Marcus,
Stan Rappaport, Dave Smith and George Van Daniker

COLUMNIST: Mike Preston

REPORTERS: Christian Ewell, Bill Free, Gary Lambrecht, Ed Lee, Don Markus,
Paul McMullen, Ken Murray and Kevin Van Valkenburg

COPY EDITORS: Simmi Buttar, Lou Cortina, Kevin Eck, Mike Farine,
Andy Knobel, Michelle Livengood, Phill McGowan, Rich McSweeney, Mike Reeb,
Ruth Sadler, Larry Tupper and Chris Zang.

EDITORIAL ASSISTANTS: Nick Brownlee, John Coffren, Jimmy McIntyre,
Colby Ware and Jeff Zrebiec

SECRETARY: Elaine Nichols